You already know the culture is going crazy, and at a pace that seems impossible to comprehend. But why? What's happening? The answer is in this book. I thank God that my friend Dr. Michael Brown has dared to say what needs saying. And I thank God for everyone who reads this vitally important explanation of where we are and what we can and must do about it.

—ERIC METAXAS
AUTHOR, *BONHOEFFER*, *MIRACLES*, AND *MARTIN LUTHER*

Having personally known Dr. Michael Brown for about four decades as a mentor and dear friend, I wholeheartedly commend this new book that brings you inspiration and revelation for these turbulent times! Read it and please encourage others to digest the rich insights Dr. Brown is bringing to us in this defining moment of America's history.

—LARRY TOMCZAK
BEST-SELLING AUTHOR AND CULTURAL COMMENTATOR

I have the utmost love and respect for Dr. Michael L. Brown. I believe I have read and reread almost all of his books. I must say, his new release, *Jezebel's War With America*, may be his most compelling. In every chapter he enters indisputable evidence in high definition that eliminates all doubt. He lays out his case as an accomplished prosecutor, and when he is done, we, the jury (reader), find Jezebel is indeed at war with America.

—JOHN KILPATRICK
SENIOR PASTOR, CHURCH OF HIS PRESENCE

Shortly before hearing about Dr. Michael Brown's book on Jezebel, I heard God in my heart say, "Study again the story of Jezebel." Jezebel is a spirit so strong, embodied in a woman in the era of the Old Testament, spoken of by Jesus, and mentioned in the book of Revelation as revisiting the earth. This is a heavy subject. It is a dangerous subject. It evokes a demonic response. It is one of hell's heroes. As I read the manuscript of this book after being invited to write an endorsement, I was moved for days. I took an inventory of my own heart. The spirit of Jezebel is active in the earth today. It comes to intimidate, control, and threaten. A study by George Barna reveals that 92 percent of pastors in America, when surveyed, stated that they say nothing in sermons about our greatest national issues. That sounds like the results of the intimidation of Jezebel. Since you have decided to read this book, get ready to be stirred. The spirit of Jezebel is back—and intends to shut up your voice of life, of freedom, of truth. The answer to overcoming this treacherous spirit is found in this book. It is timely, important, and anointed.

—Pastor Mike Hayes
Founding Pastor, Covenant Church

American culture continues to change at rapid speed, with waves of social chaos and consternation forcing many Christians to wonder how we ended up in such a dire predicament. In *Jezebel's War With America* my friend Michael L. Brown explores how spiritual elements are at play—powerful forces that can impact individuals, communities, and nations. Brown's compelling theological view gives us all a great deal to consider when it comes to truly living our faith out more fully and paving a positive path forward.

—BILLY HALLOWELL
AUTHOR, *FAULT LINE* AND *THE ARMAGEDDON CODE*

JEZEBEL'S WAR
WITH
AMERICA

MICHAEL L. BROWN, PhD

FRONT LINE

Visit the author's website at askdrbrown.org.

Library of Congress Cataloging-in-Publication Data

Names: Brown, Michael L., 1955- author.
Title: Jezebel's war with America / by Michael L. Brown, PhD.
Description: Lake Mary : FrontLine, [2019]
Identifiers: LCCN 2019014137 (print) | LCCN 2019018847 (ebook) | ISBN 9781629996677 (e-book) | ISBN 9781629996660 (hardcover) | ISBN 9781629996677 (ebk.)
Subjects: LCSH: Spiritual warfare. | United States--Moral conditions. | Jezebel, Queen, consort of Ahab, King of Israel.
Classification: LCC BV4509.5 (ebook) | LCC BV4509.5 .B763 2019 (print) | DDC 277.3/083--dc23
LC record available at https://lccn.loc.gov/2019014137

19 20 21 22 23 — 6 5 4 3 2
Printed in the United States of America

CONTENTS

PREFACE

I AM USED TO writing with a sense of urgency and burden, but I have never felt that urgency and burden any more deeply than when writing this book. In fact, about 70 percent of the book was written in a one-week period late in 2018 with the words burning inside me as I typed on my keyboard hour after hour, all day and all night. I felt fire in my heart, fire in my head, and fire in my hands.

That suggests strongly to me that the message of this book is of great importance for our nation today, that the spiritual battle is real and intense, and that we are really dealing with demonic forces that want to destroy us. But it also means we can see great victory through the Word and Spirit, in Jesus' name.

In the summer of 2018 Pastor John Kilpatrick, who was the pastor during the Brownsville Revival and who now leads a church in Daphne, Alabama, ended a Sunday service with a call to pray for President Trump. He said Trump was under attack from witchcraft and from Jezebel, something that must have sounded very odd to many when the video went viral, much to Pastor Kilpatrick's shock. Why so much attention on this call for prayer? (I share more details about this in chapter 1.)

I contacted him to encourage him for his stand, and he invited me to preach for him in October. It was then that the Lord laid the contents of this book on my heart, not as a book but as a sermon. Most of the elements for the book were in place the day I preached the message. Weeks later, in interaction with Marcos Perez and the team at Charisma House, we agreed on the need to turn the message into a full-length book, and it was then—quite suddenly and unexpectedly—that the pages began to pour out of me as quickly as I could write.

My appreciation to the entire Charisma family, including my terrific editor, Adrienne Gaines, along with Debbie Marrie, Marcos Perez, Kimberly Overcast, Steve and Joy Strang, and the rest of team, and those everywhere who faithfully pray for my ministry and the work God has called us to do. And as always, a special thanks to my bride and best friend, Nancy, for being that immovable rock of truth and conviction. We all do this together, and in Him, as one, we overcome.

So the stage is set and the battle is pitched. I say on with it, in Jesus' name!

CHAPTER 1

THE MOST WICKED WOMAN IN THE WORD OF GOD

O N AUGUST 19, 2018, at the end of his sermon, John Kilpatrick, pastor of Church of His Presence, in Daphne, Alabama, called for special prayer for President Trump.[1] He said witchcraft was coming against the president and quoted 2 Kings 9:22, which attributes the troubles the nation of Israel was facing to the sorceries of Jezebel.

"What's happening right now in America is witchcraft's trying to take this country over," he said. "It's witchcraft that's trying to take America back over."[2]

Pastor Kilpatrick is a dear friend and a very serious man of God. We served together when he was the pastor of Brownsville Assembly, which hosted the Brownsville Revival, a move of God that continued without interruption from 1995 to 2000. He went on to be used by God in another major outpouring several years later. He is not a man given to hype or exaggeration.

"I am not being political," he told his congregation, "but…here's what the Holy Spirit said to me last night, and here's what He said for me to tell you. He said, 'Tell the church that so far Trump has been dealing with Ahab. But Jezebel's fixing to step out from the shadows.' That's what the Lord said to me.…He said, 'Pray for him now because,' He said, 'there's about to be a shift, and the deep state is about to manifest, and it's going to be a showdown like you can't believe.' So I'm coming to you as a prophet, as a man of God, and I'm telling you, it's time to pray for the president."[3]

To Pastor Kilpatrick's complete surprise, the video of his call for prayer went viral, and within two days the president was under extreme attack. The story about Pastor Kilpatrick's call for prayer was covered by Christian and secular media, including even the *Jerusalem Post*,[4] in which the coverage was remarkably fair.

The word God gave Pastor Kilpatrick clearly struck a nerve, and I can say it resonated with my spirit immediately. But why? What does Jezebel have to do with Donald Trump, who is hardly a prophet of God? And in what sense is witchcraft trying to take over America? What might the Holy Spirit be speaking to the church in this season, and what is at stake if we fail to respond?

I will answer those questions and more as we move through the pages of this book. But before we can understand why Jezebel is stepping out of the shadows, we must discover who exactly Jezebel is.

THE WOMAN JEZEBEL

Without question Jezebel was the most wicked woman in the Bible. She was an idol-worshipping seductress who slaughtered God's prophets, terrified His servants, had her enemies assassinated, and emasculated her husband, the king of Israel. She stands as the epitome of an evil woman.

Her husband, Ahab, was already an ungodly man before they married, but his marriage to Jezebel caused him to surpass the wickedness of the previous kings of Israel. She was the unholy spark that ignited a destructive, deadly fire.

As recorded in 1 Kings 16:29–31:

> In the thirty-eighth year of Asa king of Judah, Ahab the son of Omri began to reign over Israel, and Ahab the son of Omri reigned over Israel in Samaria twenty-two years. Ahab the son of Omri did more evil in the sight of the LORD than all who were before him. The sins of Jeroboam[5] the son of Nebat were seen as minor

for him to walk in, for he took Jezebel the daughter of Ethbaal, king of the Sidonians, as his wife and went and served Baal and worshipped him.

It is little surprise, then, that the name Jezebel has become proverbial, as in "She's such a Jezebel!" As explained in the online Urban Dictionary, Jezebel is:

A female who is seeking attention from and possibly plotting to use someone who is wealthy or otherwise desirable in order to gain status in society.

She is often beautiful and knows it, she uses her looks to her advantage to "lure in" her next victim....

She will do anything and will use anyone to get what she wants. She is interested in the people she's interested in purely as a status symbol and will toss them away and move on when they no longer satisfy what she wants....

"Look at her, flirting with the best dressed guy at the bar. What a Jezebel."[6]

What exactly do we know about this evil woman Jezebel? And what was so bad about Ahab's marrying her in the first place?

Let's start with Ahab's marriage to Jezebel. It was a union between God's kingdom and the devil's, between the chosen people and the world. It was a political marriage, bringing two nations together (Israel and Sidon), even though the Lord had commanded His people *not* to intermarry with the heathen. As Moses warned the nation, "You shall not intermarry with them. You shall not give your daughters to their sons or take their daughters for your sons. For they will turn your sons away from following Me to serve other gods. Then the anger of the LORD will be inflamed against you, and He will quickly destroy you" (Deut. 7:3–4).

And that is exactly what happened. Ahab's heart was already bent on evil, but his marriage to Jezebel launched him into full-blown idolatry. He eventually brought trouble on Israel,[7] as Jezebel hardened his heart and strengthened his resolve. That's why when she underwrote the false prophets of Baal and Asherah and sought to annihilate the true prophets of Yahweh, Ahab did not resist. The two of them became cronies in crime, partners in idolatry, allies in rebellion.

But note this carefully: the Bible never says Ahab contributed to Jezebel's wickedness. It was Jezebel who helped corrupt Ahab. In fact, later in Ahab's life he expressed remorse when rebuked by a prophet, actually humbling himself and seeking God's mercy.[8] Jezebel, on her part, only became harder. The woman was given to sin, and she seduced others into apostasy. As the text says, Ahab "took Jezebel the daughter of Ethbaal, king of the Sidonians, as his wife and went and served Baal and worshipped him. He raised an altar for Baal in the house of Baal, which he had built in Samaria. Ahab made an Asherah and did more to provoke the LORD God of Israel to anger than all the kings of Israel who preceded him" (1 Kings 16:31–33).

Her gods became his gods and her sins, his sins. As the Scripture states, "There was no one like Ahab, who devoted himself to do what was evil in the LORD's sight, *because his wife Jezebel incited him*" (1 Kings 21:25, CSB, emphasis added).[9] As an ancient Jewish tradition records, "The first year that [Jezebel] entered Ahab's [home], she taught him how to serve idols."[10] And, "Who caused Ahab to be destroyed in this world and the world to come together with his sons? His wife Jezebel."[11]

What exactly do we know about Jezebel? She was the daughter of Ethbaal, king of the Sidonians (also known as the Phoenicians, located in modern-day Lebanon), meaning she was the daughter of a pagan king. But Josephus, the first-century Jewish historian, tells us Ethbaal also served as the high priest of the goddess Astarte (Ashtoreth).[12] So he was not just an idol-worshipper; he was a *devoted* idol-worshipper. (His name apparently means "with Baal."[13]) No wonder his daughter Jezebel was such a zealous devotee of false gods. She was following in the footsteps of her father.

But there's more. Biblical scholar Athalya Brenner-Idan "suggests that Phoenicia followed the Mesopotamian practice of appointing the king's daughter as the high priestess of the chief local god, in this case, Baal Melqart."[14] Summarizing Brenner-Idan's research, *The Anchor Yale Bible Dictionary* says:

> With the king as high priest and his daughter serving as high priestess, links between the monarchy and the state religion were considerably strengthened. Together, the two were able to wield substantial political, economic, and religious power over the land. Hence, when Jezebel came to Israel she was accustomed to being an active participant in government. She promoted the cult of Baal, which had long enjoyed extensive support in Israel, since her status as the god's high priestess was integral to her authority as queen.[15]

While we can't be sure that Jezebel was in fact the high priestess in the local Baal temple, there's no question about the rest, since in the ancient world there was no separation between "church" and state. For Jezebel that meant one of her goals as queen was to transform the spiritual fabric of Israel. It would not be the nation of Yahweh, the one true God. It would be the nation of idols, the nation of the Baals and the Asherahs. As queen she had the power to make this happen.

But to turn the nation away from the Lord, she had to silence the voice of God's prophets. So the next thing we read about this wicked woman is this: "And when Jezebel cut off the prophets of the LORD, Obadiah took a hundred prophets and hid them by fifties in a cave and fed them with bread and water" (1 Kings 18:4, ESV).

Look carefully at what the Hebrew text says. It does not simply say that she "killed" the prophets (see 1 Kings 18:13). It says that she "cut off" the prophets. Her goal was extermination. All opposing voices must be destroyed.

Jezebel was so successful that out of a nation of several million people there were only one hundred true prophets left, and they were reduced to hiding in caves, dependent on someone to bring them food and water. They dared not venture out, let alone speak out. To do so was to die. They were paralyzed by fear.

As for the false prophets, they were thriving, numbering eight hundred fifty combined (four hundred fifty prophets of Baal and four hundred prophets of Asherah; see 1 Kings 18:19). And all of them ate at Jezebel's table, meaning they were part of her inner circle, personally supported by the queen.

Later, we learn that the Lord still had seven thousand worshippers left in the country, seven thousand "who have not bowed their knees to Baal or kissed the images of him" (1 Kings 19:18, NET BIBLE).[16] But that was a tiny remnant among the ten tribes of Israel—seven thousand out of millions. Jezebel was firmly in control, and Ahab was with her step for step.

Only one thing—or I should say one man—stood in her path and stopped her from exerting total control: the prophet Elijah. He was absolutely fearless, telling Ahab there would be no dew or rain in Israel except according to his word, leading to a dev-astating, three-year famine. (See 1 Kings 17:1.) He even called for a public confrontation on Mount Carmel, inviting Jezebel's four hundred fifty false prophets of Baal to call down fire from heaven. When they failed after trying all day, he cried out to Yahweh, and at once the fire fell.

The people who were watching also fell—on their faces, shouting, "Yahweh, He is God! Yahweh, He is God!" (See 1 Kings 18:39.) Earlier in the day, when challenged by Elijah to decide between Yahweh and Baal, they stood silent, refusing to answer him a word. Now, overwhelmed by the divine fire, they cried out in His name. And Elijah, emboldened by the moment, seized the false prophets and put every single one of them to death as Ahab stood by and watched. (See 1 Kings 18 for the full story.)

Was there ever a bolder prophet than Elijah? Was there ever a man more full of faith and courage? Yet the Bible tells us that when Ahab told Jezebel what happened on Mount Carmel, possibly with some awe in his voice, recounting how Elijah killed all the false prophets—her very own, highly favored false prophets—Jezebel was furious. She sent a message to Elijah, saying, "So let the gods do to me and more also, if I do not make your life as the life of one of them by tomorrow about this time" (1 Kings 19:2). In other words, "Elijah, I am going to have your head!"

And how did the mighty prophet respond? *He got up and ran for his life.* Jezebel intimidated the prophet Elijah! In fact, he was so downcast that he "prayed that he might die, and said, 'It is enough! Now, LORD, take my life, for I am no better than my fathers!'" (1 Kings 19:4, NKJV). Elijah hit rock bottom. You don't mess with a woman like Jezebel without messing with your own life.

The famed preacher Charles Spurgeon theorized that Elijah became so despondent because despite the dramatic demonstration of God's power Jezebel would still rule over Ahab.[17] I personally believe there was something else going on with Elijah, something psychological and spiritual. I believe the great high on Mount Carmel was followed by a great low, that the mountaintop experience, where Elijah reached the heights of spiritual exhilaration, was followed by a dark valley, a deep emotional crash. But the fact remains that the same man who confronted the king, who took on the nation, who challenged the false prophets, who called down fire from heaven, and who killed those false prophets—Elijah, the man of God—was the same man who ran in fear from Ahab's queen, Jezebel.

THE ARCHENEMY OF THE PROPHETS

Jezebel is the archenemy of the prophets, the archenemy of true worship, the archenemy of the message of repentance. If she can't kill you, she will put you on the run as you cower in fear. If she can't exterminate you, she will intimidate you into silence. If she can't annihilate you, she will emasculate you.

So mark these words, which I do not write lightly: *If you want to be a true prophetic voice, you will have to take on Jezebel.*

Joseph Parker was a British pastor who lived from 1830 to 1902. He was a contemporary of Charles Spurgeon but not nearly as well known. Yet there is a saying of his that is as well known today as any of Spurgeon's lines. It was made famous by Leonard Ravenhill, who cited it in his classic book *Why Revival Tarries*. It was then memorialized in song by Keith Green, who read the quote in Ravenhill's book and then wrote "Pledge My Head to Heaven." Parker said this: "The man whose little sermon is 'Repent' sets himself against his age, and will for the time being be battered mercilessly by the age whose moral tone he challenges. There is but one end for such a man—'off with his head.' You had better not try to preach repentance until you have pledged your head to Heaven."[18]

In the end Elijah's words triumphed over Jezebel, and she died the gory death he prophesied.[19] But in the aftermath of his greatest prophetic victory—really, it was one of the greatest prophetic victories recorded anywhere in Scripture—Jezebel's death threat terrorized the prophet, causing him to flee and pray that he would die.

To say it again: a true prophet has no worse enemy than a woman like Jezebel. When you face her, you must pledge your head to heaven.

The next time Jezebel is mentioned is in 1 Kings 21, the story of Naboth's vineyard, and it is here that we see the stark contrast between Ahab and Jezebel. Ahab wanted to buy Naboth's property since it was right next to his own, but Naboth wouldn't sell it since it was the property of his ancestors. This caused Ahab to get depressed and sullen: "He lay down on his bed and sulked and would not eat any bread" (1 Kings 21:4).

When Jezebel found out what was going on, her response was swift: "Why in the world are you sulking? You're the king of Israel! I'll get you the vineyard." She quickly plotted against Naboth, signing letters in Ahab's name and using the king's seal, inviting Naboth to sit at a place of honor in a prominent fast. She then hired false witnesses to accuse him of speaking against God and the king. As a result he was stoned to death on the spot, and Jezebel told Ahab, "Get up and claim the field. Naboth is dead." (See 1 Kings 21:5–16).

But when he went to claim the field, Elijah confronted him directly, prophesying his horrible death and the destruction of his posterity. Elijah also prophesied a horrible death for Jezebel.

How did Ahab respond? When he heard Elijah's words, "he tore his clothes and put on sackcloth on his flesh and fasted and lay in sackcloth and walked meekly. The word of the LORD came to Elijah the Tishbite, saying, 'See how Ahab humbles himself before Me? Because he humbles himself before Me, I will not bring the disaster during his lifetime, but during his son's lifetime I will bring the disaster on his household'" (1 Kings 21:27–29). So even wicked Ahab repented, and God had mercy on him. But Jezebel did no such thing. There was no repentance in her.

Several years go by before Jezebel is mentioned again, and by then she was no longer youthful. Ahab had died in battle about fourteen years earlier, and two of his sons had reigned as king after him. Now a new leader had arisen, Jehu, the son of Nimshi. He was about to wipe out the descendants of Ahab and become Israel's new king. He was also on a mission to destroy Jezebel. How did she respond? She tried to seduce him!

As the text states, "When Jehu came to Jezreel, Jezebel heard about it. She put black paint on her eyes, adorned her head, and looked down through the window. As Jehu entered in at the gate, she said, 'Is everything all right, Zimri, murderer of his master?'" (2 Kings 9:30–31).

She was also taunting him, calling him Zimri rather than Jehu, since Zimri, like Jehu, became king of Israel by killing the king. And Zimri only reigned for seven days. (See 1 Kings 16:9–20.) Jezebel was saying to him, "That's what will happen to you, you treasonous murderer!" But just in case he came in peace, she dolled herself up. Maybe she could control him like she controlled Ahab.

But Jehu was not to be controlled. He was the ultimate overzealous alpha male, the proverbial bull in the china shop, doing almost as much harm as good. Within minutes Jezebel was dead, her body eaten by dogs. In Jehu's own words, she was guilty of "countless harlotries and sorceries" (2 Kings 9:22, JPS TANAKH).

That is what we know about this wicked woman Jezebel, a woman who died almost three thousand years ago. And yet in a very real way the influence of the same demonic forces that worked through her are still being felt today in twenty-first-century America.

We see it in the massive increase of pornography and sexual temptation. We see it in the militant spirit of abortion, which ties in with pagan idolatry. We see it in the rise of radical feminism, which is dead set against all male authority. We see it in the new fascination with sorcery and witchcraft. And we see it in the attempt to silence prophetic voices in the land. Her schemes may look a little different, but Jezebel has the same mission: to transform the spiritual fabric of the nation and turn us away from God.

Interestingly, just as Jezebel was on a collision course with Jehu, the bull-in-a-china-shop king of Israel, the spirit of Jezebel is on a collision course with Donald Trump, the bull-in-a-china-shop president of the United States. His presidency, for better or worse, has mobilized millions of proabortion, anti-male feminists who rage in the streets, calling for his death and (literally) pounding on the doors of congressional buildings in protest of his pro-life court appointees.[20]

The battle is being waged, and Jezebel, in a sense, is back from the dead. Or perhaps the spirit of Jezebel never went away.

CHAPTER 2

JEZEBEL IS ALIVE AND WELL IN AMERICA TODAY

Almost one thousand years after the death of Jezebel, Jesus Himself referred to her again, but this time it was a different woman called by the same name. Speaking to the church of Thyatira in the Book of Revelation, Jesus first commended the congregation for the good it was doing before delivering these shocking words:

> But I have a few things against you: You permit that woman Jezebel, who calls herself a prophetess, to teach and seduce My servants to commit sexual immorality and eat food sacrificed to idols. I gave her time to repent of her sexual immorality, but she did not repent. Look! I will throw her onto a sickbed, and those who commit adultery with her into great tribulation, unless they repent of their deeds. I will put her children to death, and all the churches shall know that I am He who searches the hearts and minds. I will give to each one of you according to your deeds.
>
> —REVELATION 2:20–23

Jezebel was at it again, seducing, deceiving, and destroying. And she was doing it right inside the church. This was intolerable to the Lord, and the judgment He promised was intense.

Who was this so-called prophetess? We have no definitive record other than what is recorded here, but it's likely that her name was not really Jezebel. Instead, most scholars believe Jesus gave her this name *because she was just like the Jezebel of old.* She was a woman of the same spirit, operating by the same demonic forces, turning God's people away from the truth into sexual immorality and idolatry. In that sense Jezebel has appeared on the scene over and over again throughout history, right until this day.

So there is Jezebel the woman, the wife of Ahab and the daughter of a pagan king. That woman is long dead. And there is Jezebel the spirit, meaning the demonic power that acted through her and through her New Testament counterpart. That spirit is still alive and thriving.

Put another way, we know that human beings are fully responsible for their actions and cannot say, "The devil made me do it!" But we also know that Satan is our ultimate enemy, the one with whom we do battle. As Paul wrote, "For our fight is not against flesh and blood, but against principalities, against powers, against the rulers of the darkness of this world, and against spiritual forces of evil in the heavenly places" (Eph. 6:12). That's why Jezebel had such power. She was not simply a domineering, manipulative woman. She was demonically empowered as well—hence her almost supernatural ability to intimidate and control. And when we see this same type of demonic activity at work in our day, we identify it as the spirit of Jezebel.

This doesn't mean there is a specific demon (or principality) named Jezebel.[1] It means there are certain characteristics associated with Jezebel, and when we see this same set of characteristics at work, we know who is behind it. Put another way, when we observe the same things happening in our society (or within the church) as happened in Israel in Jezebel's day, we understand it is no coincidence. It is satanic, it is systematic, and it is intentional. And that's why I say *Jezebel is alive and well today in twenty-first-century America.*

On a certain level even the world recognizes this, as witnessed by the modern feminist website named Jezebel (Jezebel .com). As noted on the Media Research Center (MRC) website,

"Feminism isn't just a brutal philosophy for millions of unborn children. It's brutal on the internet. Take the website Jezebel .com, a reference to the prophetess in the Book of Revelation who was 'teaching and beguiling my servants to practice immorality.'"[2]

So radical feminists decided to launch a website and what name did they choose? Jezebel! Is anyone surprised? A tweet encouraging people to subscribe to their newsletter offers this: "Gender, culture, and politics. With teeth. Delivered straight to your inbox."[3] As expected!

The MRC also noted that the website had been turned into *The Book of Jezebel*, calling it "a snark-loaded feminist encyclopedia." For instance, it describes the condom as "a must-have accessory for protection against two potentially life-threatening conditions: AIDS (among other STIs) and babies."[4] The full title is *The Book of Jezebel: An Illustrated Encyclopedia of Lady Things*, and the dedication reads: "For All the Jezebels, biblical and otherwise."[5] And what exactly is in this book? The MRC article offers some samples:

> "Children" are defined as the "side effect of sex."...A "zygote" is "too young to be a slut, so way more entitled to civil rights than you are."

> The *Jezebel* entry for "misogyny" is "Exemplified by God, Aristotle, Phyllis Schlafly, Rush Limbaugh, The Republican Party, Allen West."[6]

As for the entry on "God" in *The Book of Jezebel*, it reads:

> His books overflow with misogynist messages. In Genesis, the first woman is created from a man's rib,

has a weakness for snakes and fruit, and is responsible for destroying the blissful Garden of Eden. In the New Testament, the Immaculate Conception creates the impossible and unbearable Madonna/whore dichotomy our society still suffers under today.[7]

Yes, according to this feminist compilation, God Himself appears on a list they have titled "A Rogue's Gallery of Wretched Misogynists." Jezebel lives on.

A WOMAN OF IDOLATRY AND SORCERY

Now, let's go back to the Bible and review what we learned about this wicked woman so far. We saw in the last chapter that she was:

- a zealous idol worshipper (who in the New Testament also claimed to be a prophetess)

- a seductress

- an archenemy of the prophets

- a murderer

- a woman who emasculated her husband

- a woman who engaged in sorcery

If we break this down some more, a very clear picture emerges.

The primary deities Ahab and Jezebel worshipped were Baal (male) and Asherah (female). According to Canaanite myth, Baal (whose name means "master, lord"[8]) was the son of El, the chief deity (whose name means "god"[9]), and his wife Asherah. Baal was a weather deity, which also meant he was associated with the fertility of the land, while Asherah was the fertility goddess par excellence.

Bible teacher Ray Vander Laan notes that "Baal is portrayed as a man with the head and horns of a bull, an image similar to that in biblical accounts. His right hand (sometimes both hands) is raised, and he holds a lightning bolt, signifying both destruction and fertility." As for Asherah, "she is portrayed as a nude female, sometimes pregnant, with exaggerated [or multiple] breasts that she holds out, apparently as symbols of the fertility she promises her followers."[10]

As for the worship of Asherah, Vander Laan writes:

> Although she was believed to be Baal's mother, she was also his mistress. Pagans practiced "sympathetic magic", that is, they believed they could influence the gods' actions by performing the behavior they wished the gods to demonstrate. Believing the sexual union of Baal and Asherah produced fertility, their worshippers engaged in immoral sex to cause the gods to join together, ensuring good harvests. This practice became the basis for religious prostitution (1 Kings 14:23–24).[11]

As for the worship of Baal, he notes that "at times of crisis, Baal's followers sacrificed their children, apparently the first-born of the community, to gain personal prosperity."[12]

Now, we know from other biblical texts that the abhorrent practice of child sacrifice was associated in particular with the god Molech (Lev. 18:21; 20:2–5; 2 Kings 23:10). But Molech worship, along with passing children through the fire, was also associated with Baal: "They built the high places of Baal in the Valley of the Son of Hinnom, to offer up their sons and daughters to Molech, though I did not command them, nor did it enter into my mind, that they should do this abomination, to cause Judah to sin" (Jer. 32:35, ESV; see also Jer. 19:5, which only mentions sacrificing children to Baal, without any reference to Molech).[13]

A number of passages confirm that child sacrifice was associated with other gods as well. As Moses instructed Israel, "You shall not worship the LORD your God in that way [meaning as the Canaanites do]; for every abomination to the LORD which He hates they have done to their gods; for they burn even their sons and daughters in the fire *to their gods*" (Deut. 12:31, NKJV, emphasis added; see also Deut. 18:9–10; 2 Kings 16:3; 21:6; Jer. 7:31; Ezek. 16:21). As one commentator notes, "Such unspeakable forms of religious expression were common in the ancient Near Eastern world, especially in Canaan, and tragically enough sometimes were emulated by God's own elect nation."[14]

We don't know whether Jezebel encouraged this practice, but we do know that child sacrifice was intimately connected with pagan idolatry. And to the extent idolatry was practiced by the people of Israel and Judah, child sacrifice was often practiced as well. Later in the book you will read an absolutely shocking account of how these children were sacrificed. (They were quite literally burned alive.) But suffice it to say here that baby killing and idol worship were closely connected in ancient Israel.

Idolatry was also closely associated with sexual immorality in the Old Testament. That's why we read descriptions like this: "While Israel dwelt in Shittim, the people began to commit harlotry with the women of Moab. They called the people to the sacrifices of their gods, and the people ate and bowed down to their gods. Israel joined himself to the Baal of Peor, and the anger of the LORD was inflamed against Israel" (Num. 25:1–3).

Likewise, looking back at this same incident, Moses notes that the Moabite women "caused the children of Israel, through the word of Balaam, to act unfaithfully against the LORD concerning the thing of Peor, and there was a plague among the assembly of the LORD" (Num. 31:16).

So not only was Jezebel a seductress—remember Jehu's reference to her "harlotries" in 2 Kings 9:22—but sexual immorality and idolatry went hand in hand. Are you starting to see a pattern? Jezebel was associated with sexual immorality and idolatry, and idolatry was associated with baby killing. This is why I say that Jezebel is alive and well in America today.

Not only so, but Jezebel was the ultimate feminist. I mean this in terms of radical feminism, in contrast with a healthy appreciation of women and a desire for them to be treated equally and fairly. To Jezebel, men were to be used as a means to an end, and in her marriage it's clear who wore the pants.

So in conjunction with Jezebel and her idolatry, we have sexual immorality, baby killing, and radical feminism. Does this sound like America today? Pornography has become a plague, and immorality is celebrated. Baby killers have become more militant by the day, determined to preserve their "right" to terminate children in the womb. And radical feminism has declared war on "male patriarchy," with tens of thousands marching down our streets in protest.

Yet there's still more. Jehu also referenced Jezebel's "sorceries" in 2 Kings 9:22, using the Hebrew word *kesheph*, which some translations render as "witchcraft."[15] Regardless, though, of which word is used, we know sorcery and witchcraft are closely related concepts. We also know sorcery and witchcraft are on the rise in America today.[16]

Is it any surprise, then, that we also see a frontal assault on the prophetic message today? That the preaching of repentance and the call to turn from sin are so firmly resisted? That there is a concerted effort from many sides to snuff out the prophetic voice of the church? The same demonic powers that operated through Jezebel in the Old Testament and Jezebel in the New Testament are at work again today. In fact, you could even say they have shifted into overdrive. Jezebel is thriving.

ENCOUNTERING JEZEBEL FIRSTHAND

On three different occasions I had direct encounters with this Jezebel-type demonic power. On two of the occasions the battle lasted for several months; the other occasion was just for weeks. But I can tell you firsthand that each time was miserable. As I noted in one journal entry, "What fierce, tormenting oppression!" During those times, it felt like I was running through knee-deep water, with spiritual resistance on every front. And I knew this was a direct, Jezebelian attack on the prophetic message the Lord had given me for the nation.

The first time I encountered this demonic power, it was as if all hell broke loose against my wife, Nancy, and me. She came under sudden and bizarre health attacks. We felt constant pressure—even oppression—on our lives. We were both bombarded by lies, demonically planted thoughts that sought to destroy each of us from a different angle. (We only realized the depth of this after the fact, when things really came to light spiritually.) Even ministry became a total drag for me.

I had been preaching since I was eighteen, starting in 1973, and I loved to travel and minister the Word. But during that season of attack I dreaded it. I didn't want to get on the plane. I didn't want to stand behind the pulpit. The warfare was like nothing I had ever experienced, and I had to pray for several hours at a time just to get to the starting line.

Above all I felt spiritually emasculated—not by a person but by some demonic power. I felt intimidated. I was hit by fears. I felt a constant challenge against bringing any type of prophetic message, and it was easy to understand what was happening. All this was totally unusual for me. "This is just like Jezebel and Elijah!" I thought to myself. (Lest anyone misunderstand me, I was not comparing myself to Elijah. I was thinking about how Jezebel attacked and intimidated those with a prophetic message, and at that time, God had birthed a prophetic message of repentance for the nation in my heart.)

By God's grace, and after serious, extended prayer, coupled with fasting and a prophetic word from a colleague, the stronghold was broken. But, to repeat, it was miserable. Nancy would affirm this as well.

Then, while traveling with Nancy and a small team in India, I encountered this Jezebelian spirit again. We were preparing to minister in the city of Vijayawada in Andhra Pradesh, and my Indian colleague and I had a burden to confront the idol worshipped by millions in that state. It was a female deity named Kanaka Durga, whose big temple was housed on a mountain in that city. God had put a message in my heart to invite the Hindu priests and the worshippers of this idol to have a public service asking who the real god was, Kanaka Durga or Yahweh. (I didn't do this lightly; I felt God put it in my heart.)

We were in India for about one month, and as we got closer to our time in Vijayawada, I began to feel that same type of oppression, something very similar to what I experienced almost five years earlier. I felt emasculated spiritually. I felt I had no authority. I felt intimidated by the challenge of preaching against idolatry. Shades of Jezebel once again!

I asked my colleague, Brother Yesupadam, to tell me a little about this goddess. What did her statue look like? And was there anything unusual about the worship associated with her?

He described this powerful, false deity as a warrior goddess with multiple arms, holding the head of a giant she had conquered in one of her hands. He also told me that once a year, her male worshippers would put on women's clothes and wear makeup. Seriously! Talk about an intimidating, emasculating, demonic image.

When I subsequently researched things for myself, I learned that this warrior goddess was depicted as a beautiful woman. (Remember how seductive Jezebel was?) But she rode on the back of a fierce lion, holding a spear in one of her many hands. What my friend described as the head of a giant was actually the image of the demon king Mahishasura, whom Kanaka Durga vanquished, according to Hindu myth. In the image I'm looking at now, the spear has pierced his side, which is gushing blood, as he looks back over his shoulder with fear at his conqueror.[17]

This is what I was encountering in the spirit—a demonic entity, represented in Hindu myth by this goddess. And it was so reminiscent of my earlier encounter with this Jezebelian type of satanic power.

Because our itinerary was so packed, we would do three meetings a day for three days, then on some occasions immediately get on our little, non-air-conditioned bus with the luggage tied to the top of the vehicle and drive all night to the next location. The schedule itself was brutal. But it was also glorious, as we saw Jesus exalted in every city.

When it came time to travel to Vijayawada, we were able to get a few hours of sleep after our night meeting before leaving the next morning while it was still dark. Because I didn't want to wake Nancy, when I got out of bed to start to get our things ready, I didn't turn the lights on in our little room, trying to make my way in the darkness. Suddenly I felt a shooting pain in my right heel. What was *that*? It turns out that I had scraped the back of my foot against the ragged, wooden edge of a bedpost, and the flesh, about the size of a quarter, was literally ripped off. Ouch!

Immediately I heard Genesis 3:15 in my spirit, applied afresh to that moment: he (meaning the enemy of our souls, the devil) will bruise your heel, but you will crush his head. (See Romans 16:20.) I knew we would have victory over Kanaka Durga, and with the Spirit's enablement we did. The Lord's name was mightily glorified in Vijayawada, a demonized man began to dance in a way that was humiliating and confess that Kanaka Durga was a not a true god, and many Hindus were powerfully touched.

But once again I saw how real this demonic opposition was—what we have described as the same type of demonic powers that operated through Queen Jezebel—and how this power could be vanquished in Jesus' name.

The third time I encountered this demonic power came as I was teaching and preaching on the theme of Jesus revolution. The message was simple: Jesus changes us, so we will go in His power and change the world. This is not a religion; it is a revolution. But before we can see gospel revolution in the society, there must first be revolution in the church, meaning, the Lord helping us recover our biblical foundations.[18]

In response to this message another hellish attack came against me. Satan really wanted to take me out, and the battle was intense, ebbing and flowing for many months until final, glorious, wonderful victory came. Jezebel—not a person but a demonic power—lost again, but the test was severe.

Of course the Lord also used these times to bring me to a place of deeper surrender and obedience, purging my flesh with His holy fire. But to this day I do not treat the subject of Jezebel lightly. The battle is real, and it is not for the faint of heart. And to this day, if Jezebel can silence the prophets, she can turn a nation's heart.

Jezebel continues to seduce and deceive. Let's examine how she is using the spirit of idolatry that is sweeping through our country.

CHAPTER 3

JEZEBEL AND IDOLATRY

ALTHOUGH JEZEBEL COMMITTED all kinds of evil acts, it was her idolatry that made her who she was. The worship of false gods moved her and molded her, and the evil that poured out of her heart flowed straight from her misplaced worship. Even now Jezebel wants to turn our hearts away from the one true God because *we become like the ones we worship and adore.*

There's a striking passage in Psalm 115 that says this all so clearly:

> Not unto us, O LORD, not unto us, but unto Your name give glory, for the sake of Your mercy, and for the sake of Your truth.
>
> Why should the nations say, "Where now is their God?" But our God is in the heavens; He does whatever He pleases. Their idols are silver and gold, the work of men's hands. They have mouths, but they cannot speak; eyes, but they cannot see; they have ears, but they cannot hear; noses, but they cannot smell; they have hands, but they cannot feel; feet, but they cannot walk; neither can they speak with their throat. *Those who make them are like them; so is everyone who trusts in them.*
>
> —PSALM 115:1–8, EMPHASIS ADDED

The people of the nations were spiritually blind, deaf, and dumb; morally crippled and handicapped. This was because the gods they worshipped were spiritually blind, deaf, and dumb; they were morally crippled and handicapped. Have you ever seen a piece of wood speak or a carved rock sing or a cast-metal statue jump and run? Just as the idols were powerless, so were those who worshipped them. Just as the false gods were evil, so were their followers.

One of the most famous Jewish traditions tells us how Abraham, whose father, Terah, was an idol worshipper,[1] was able to open his father's eyes. The story goes like this:

> Rabbi Hiyya the grandson of Rabbi Adda of Yaffo [said]: Terah was a worshipper of idols. One time he had to travel to a place, and he left Abraham in charge of his store. When a man would come in to buy [idols], Abraham would ask: How old are you? They would reply: fifty or sixty. Abraham would then respond: Woe to him who is sixty years old and worships something made today—the customer would be embarrassed, and would leave. A woman entered carrying a dish full of flour. She said to him: this is for you, offer it before them. Abraham took a club in his hands and broke all of the idols, and placed the club in the hands of the biggest idol. When his father returned, he asked: who did all of this? Abraham replied: I can't hide it from you—a woman came carrying a dish of flour and told me to offer it before them. I did, and one of them said 'I will eat it first,' and another said 'I will eat it first.' The biggest one rose, took a club, and smashed the rest of them. Terah said: what, do you think you can trick me? They don't have cognition! Abraham said: Do your ears hear what your mouth is saying?[2]

Once, while preaching in a village in India, I told this same story. (The people listening were Hindus and therefore idol worshippers. It is commonly said that there are thirty-three million gods in Hinduism![3]) They smiled as they heard the story, recognizing there was truth to the account. I also illustrated it for them by kicking a tree and pointing out how the tree did not respond because it was a tree. Then I asked them, "So if I took this tree, cut out a piece of it, and made it into an idol, does it now have power? Should I now worship it?"

Of course, Hindu teachers would tell me I'm misunderstanding their faith and that these wooden idols are representations of various manifestations of deity. But the people listening certainly got the point. As for the Indian Christians with me, the Abraham story became the talk of the day. What a great illustration of the powerlessness of false gods!

But there's actually more that needs to be said, since the story illustrates the *folly* of idolatry but does not illustrate the *evil* of idolatry. As Paul explained in 1 Corinthians 10:20, when pagans offer a sacrifice to an idol, "what the pagans sacrifice is to demons and not to God, and I don't want you to become partners with demons" (TLV). That's why idolatry opens the floodgates of evil. When we worship idols and give ourselves to them, we become *partners with demons*. What a frightful thought. And what an explanation of Jezebel's evil ways. Talk about being a partner of the devil!

You see, when we worship the one true God, we come under His power, under His influence. We worship Him for who He is—glorious, holy, just, true, pure, and compassionate. And as we read His Word, as we bask in His presence in worship, as His Spirit works in our lives, we are conformed to His character, and He carries out His work on earth through us. The same thing happens with the worship of idols. Those who worship these false gods become like them. Those who worship idols become partners with demonic forces. Those who worship them become demonized themselves.

On another trip to India we were driving down the road when we passed a group of Hindu worshippers marching on the side of the street. It was one of the ghastliest sights I've ever seen, hardly the norm even in Hinduism. The men looked like ghouls, like the walking dead. Their eyes were glazed—they seemed to be in a trance—and they were pierced through different parts of their bodies, with long pins going right through their tongues. Talk about demonic! Talk about dark and deadly. This was a real-life personification of the depravity of idolatry. This was an act of worship?

Recently an Indian leader took exception to a similar abusive practice that has become popular in India. She wrote on her blog:

> Parents conspire with temple authorities to put their children through rigorous mental and physical abuse for five days....And on the final day, each of them will be decked up with yellow clothes, garlands, jewellery and makeup on face including lipstick and made to stand in a queue for their last unexpected torture. An iron hook, tiny though it is, will be pierced into their skin on their flanks. They scream. Blood comes out. A thread will be symbolically knotted through the hooks to symbolise their bond with divinity. Then hooks are pulled out and ash roughly applied on the wounds! All this for temple deity![4]

This is part of spiritual devotion? This pleases the deity? Only when the deity is a demon.

A SOLDIER OF SATAN

David Berkowitz was one of the most notorious serial killers in New York, terrorizing the city for several years as the "Son of Sam." Years later, in prison, he received forgiveness and new life in Jesus, and he has been a witness to many since then while serving out the rest of his days behind bars.[5] Although he takes full responsibility for his crimes, even writing to the governor once to say he did not deserve parole, David will tell you plainly where he received his inspiration to kill his innocent victims: Satan himself.

In 2013, Scott Bonn, PhD, then assistant professor of sociology and criminology at Drew University in Madison, New Jersey, spent five hours interviewing David for a book he was working on. It was devoted to understanding "why so many people are fascinated with serial killers and the dark side of mankind."[6] Professor Bonn believes David acted alone (contrary to some claims that others killed with him), but he notes, "It is true that he became obsessed with the occult and worshipped Satan prior to his murders." Bonn also writes, David "felt like 'a soldier on a mission' when he went out to kill. He was convinced that Satan would set him free of his emotional pain and loneliness through the act of murder. Instead, despite some initial euphoria, each murder left David feeling empty and unfulfilled."[7]

He continues:

> Contrary to popular belief, David is not mentally ill....*I believe that he was driven to kill by his obsession with Satan and the occult....*[After his release from the Army] David turned to the occult for meaning and purpose in his empty life. By 1976, the occult had

become a complete obsession with him. I believe that David became like a drug addict in his serial murders, believing that each one would finally provide relief from loneliness and despair that he desperately sought. It never came.[8]

The devil is a murderer, and those who worship him become like him. To this day David sounds the alarm about satanism. It is not some harmless game.

It's also true, though, that the devil is very clever, that he works with subtlety, that he does not seduce and destroy overnight. If he did, many people would resist and flee. They wanted a little fun, a little stimulation. They were willing to experiment. But they weren't about to sacrifice a child to the devil on a ritual altar or become demented serial killers. No way.

That's why the enemy normally doesn't come in through the front door. He finds another opening, a back door just a little bit ajar (I'm speaking metaphorically here) or a window not tightly closed, and next thing he's in our living room. Then little by little he reveals his evil ways. Little by little he desensitizes our consciences. Little by little he takes us captive. And before long we are his slaves.

On a very large scale this is what has happened to our nation, and what Paul described about the human race in Romans 1 can be applied to us today. I'll reword the text for effect, making it about our nation—us!—rather than humanity as a whole. Paul wrote (with a change of subjects here from "they" to "we"):

Because, although we once knew God, we did not glorify Him or give thanks to Him as God, but became futile in our imaginations, and our foolish hearts were darkened. Claiming to be wise, we became fools. We changed the glory of the incorruptible God into an image made like corruptible man, birds, four-footed beasts, and creeping things.

Therefore God gave us up to uncleanness through the lusts of our hearts, to dishonor our own bodies among ourselves. We turned the truth of God into a lie and worshipped and served the creature rather than the Creator, who is blessed forever. Amen.

—ROMANS 1:21–25, MODIFIED

Does this sound familiar? Isn't this exactly what we have done in America, turning from our Bible-based foundations and becoming a nation of idolaters? And what does Paul say in the verses that follow? Because humanity (but I'll say "we" again here, speaking of the United States) would not repent, God turned us over to abuses of His design for us, with men having sex with men and with women having sex with women. And, he writes, we received in ourselves "the due penalty of our error" (Rom. 1:27, modified).

What came next?

And since we did not see fit to acknowledge God, God gave us over to a debased mind, to do those things which are not proper. We were filled with all unrighteous-ness, sexual immorality, wickedness, covetousness, maliciousness; full of envy, murder, strife, deceit. We are gossips, slanderers, God-haters, insolent, proud, boastful, inventors of evil things, and disobedient toward parents, without understanding, covenant breakers, without natural affection, calloused, and unmerciful, who know the righteous requirement of God, that those who commit such things are worthy of death. We not only do them, but also give hearty approval to those who practice them.

—ROMANS 1:28–32, MODIFIED

Does this accurately describe America today? There is much good in our midst, to be sure. There are tens of millions of born-again believers, and many are living godly lives. But overall we are corrupt. We are filled with lust. We are consumed with greed. We bow to the gods of carnal entertainment, of fanatical obsession with sports, of fleshly fashion, of empty intellectual pride. Atheism is a growing religion in our midst. Alternate forms of spirituality abound. And while the great majority of the nation still professes to be Christian, many have become idolaters instead.

Even in some of our "gospel preaching" churches, by which I mean churches that hold to the orthodox fundamentals of the faith, our message has become mixed with idolatry. The Lord is not the center of attention. We are.

We think we are not here to serve Him; He is here to serve us. And if it doesn't feel good *to us*, if it doesn't sync with *our desires*, if it's not in conformity with *our will*, then it's certainly not from Him.

More than seventy years ago, in his classic article "The Old Cross and the New," A. W. Tozer wrote, "The old cross would have no truck with the world. For Adam's proud flesh it meant the end of the journey." In contrast, he noted with profound insight, "The new cross does not slay the sinner, it redirects him."[9] Today we could take this one step further and say, "The new cross does not slay sinners; it empowers them."

So the message goes: Jesus came to make you into a bigger and better you! Jesus came to help you fulfill your dreams and your destiny! The gospel is all about you!

Our contemporary "gospel" says, "This is who I am, this is how I feel, and God is here to please me." This is a form of idolatry. The biblical gospel says, "This is who God is, this is how He feels, and we are here to please Him." The difference between these two messages is the difference between heaven and hell.

Let's listen to Dr. Tozer again as he describes the essence of idolatry:

> Among the sins to which the human heart is prone, hardly any other is more hateful to God than idolatry, for idolatry is at bottom a libel on His character. The idolatrous heart assumes God is other than He is—in itself a monstrous sin—and substitutes for the true God one made after its own likeness. Always this God will conform to the image of the one who created it and will be base or pure, cruel or kind, according to the moral state of the mind from which it emerges.[10]

So there is a sinful cycle here, a cycle of death. Human beings, out of the evil of their hearts, create a god in their own image. But then, as we have seen, this god becomes empowered by demons, which in turn drive the idol worshippers deeper into sin and depravity.

Tozer then makes this important observation:

> Let us beware lest we in our pride accept the erroneous notion that idolatry consists only in kneeling before visible objects of adoration, and that civilized

peoples are therefore free from it. The essence of idolatry is the entertainment of thoughts about God that are unworthy of Him. It begins in the mind and may be present where no overt act of worship has taken place. "When they knew God," wrote Paul, "they glorified him not as God, neither were thankful; but became vain in their imaginations, and their foolish heart was darkened."[11]

These are sobering words. We might not be worshipping at the altar of some Hindu deity. We might not be piercing our tongues with steel rods. (Did I mention that those demonic marchers I saw in India were not bleeding at all, despite all their piercings?) We might not be listening to the voice of Satan and becoming serial killers. But as our hearts drift from the worship of the one true God, they inevitably go the way of idolatry, of deception, of the flesh.

Tozer concludes with this:

Then followed the worship of idols fashioned after the likeness of men and birds and beasts and creeping things. But this series of degrading acts began in the mind. Wrong ideas about God are not only the fountain from which the polluted waters of idolatry flow; they are themselves idolatrous. The idolater simply imagines things about God and acts as if they were true.[12]

A LESSON FROM MOUNT SINAI

Do you remember what happened when Moses was on Mount Sinai? The people of Israel became weary of waiting for him to return—after all, he was away for forty days without any communication—and they wanted Aaron to make them a physical representation of God, something they could look at and worship and offer sacrifices to. So Aaron complied and made a golden calf. But that was hardly the end of the story.

As Exodus tells us, once the calf was erected, "they rose up early on the next day, and offered burnt offerings, and brought peace offerings. And the people sat down to eat and to drink, and rose up to play" (Exod. 32:6). And play they did, offering their sacrifices, dancing (see Exod. 32:19), and who knows what else. Rabbinic interpretation of the word *play* claims that it implies sexual sin. As expressed by the famed rabbi known as Rashi (1040–1105), "There is implied in this term besides idolatry also sexual immorality."[13]

It was at this moment that Moses, along with Joshua, made his way down from Mount Sinai. He had been warned by the Lord that Israel had fallen headlong into sin, breaking the very first commandment, which was a prohibition of idolatry.

> When Joshua heard the noise of the people as they shouted, he said to Moses, "There is a sound of war in the camp."
> But he said: "It is not the sound of those who shout for victory, nor is it the sound of those who cry because of being overcome, but I hear the sound of singing."
> —Exodus 32:17–18

The people were in all-out party mode. *Having cast off the one true God, by creating a god in earthly form, they also cast off restraint.*

Can you picture this in your mind? Multiplied thousands of people shouting and dancing, out of control. (Picture a modern-day rave, which I've seen from a distance on YouTube, and it might have looked like that.) Maybe they were drinking too. Maybe they were having orgies. Either way, it was a dark and demonic scene, even though they were doing it in the name of Yahweh.

Now, step back and look at our nation today. It too is filled with idolatry. The people have cast off restraint. So much drunkenness. So much drug abuse. So much gluttony. So much sexual sin. So much perversion. So much violence. So little focused, truly devoted adoration of the Lord. So little purity.

And just look at our passions and lusts. During football season in America there is far more passion expressed for the NFL than for the Lord. (Do you think I'm exaggerating? If so, tell me the last time you saw people as ecstatic or as grieved in God's house as at a football stadium or watching the game on TV.) And what about our lust *for things*? According to Paul, "covetousness...is idolatry" (Col. 3:5). Almost every ad on TV is designed to get us to covet. And the list goes on and on. (In the next chapter we'll see how deeply sexual immorality is connected to idolatry.)

A NATION OF IDOLATERS

Shortly after Richard Wurmbrand emigrated from Romania following fourteen years of brutal imprisonment for his faith, he was speaking at a home meeting in Minnesota. When the meeting ended, one of the men present asked Pastor Wurmbrand, "Why is it that we don't have to deal with communism here in America?"

This was an important question! After all, Wurmbrand had suffered unspeakable agony because of the communists, and his wife, Sabina, had languished in a slave labor camp for years, separated from her husband and their son. Some of their best friends and colleagues had been killed for their faith, while others had been tortured and endured hardships beyond description. Why had America been spared the horrors of communism? Why had the church here escaped the fury of atheistic persecution? How did Pastor Wurmbrand respond?

We might have expected him to say, "It is because of your national heritage! It is because you have not built or accepted a communist government, because there are too many believers in your country to allow such a thing to happen, because the church has consistently cried out to God." Yes, he could well have responded like this, and to a great extent, he would have been correct. But that was not his answer. Instead he replied, "You don't have communism here; you have something far worse. You have materialism!"

What chilling, unsettling words! Materialism worse than communism? Materialism a greater menace to the church than atheistic persecution? How can this be?[14]

As I write these words, my mind's eye goes from a picture of Israel partying at the golden calf to a picture of America—the whole nation, crowded from coast to coast—and it is throbbing and pulsating and bobbing with masses of people partying, others frantically running here and there, and others giving themselves to the flesh. But there is very little holy worship ascending to the throne, very little time for God, very little separation, very little reflection, very little devotion. The partying crowds rule the day, and holy service to the Lord fits in wherever it can, often as another form of entertainment.

As I saw this internal vision, a message was shouting to me. Are we not a nation of idolaters? Isn't this the first sign that Jezebel has her hooks in our land? And isn't this the first giant step into a host of other sins, from immorality to baby killing, from radical feminism to the war on gender, from witchcraft to the silencing of the prophets? Aren't these all connected, and don't they all flow from the polluted stream of idolatry?

My friends, Jezebel is not coming. She is here. And she is happy with what she sees. Idolatry is rampant in the land. The door of hell has been opened on America. If it's not shut quickly, our complete moral and spiritual collapse will soon follow.

My heart burns to see a spiritual awakening unlike anything the nation has seen—the greatest awakening we have ever experienced. But we'd better get desperate if we want to see God move.

CHAPTER 4

JEZEBEL AND THE SEXUAL SEDUCTION OF AMERICA

HERE IS NOTHING new about sexual immorality. It has been here throughout human history, which is why the Bible frequently addresses sexual sin. One of the Ten Commandments states, "You shall not commit adultery" (Exod. 20:14). Jesus warned that sexual immorality could damn us to hell (Matt. 5:27–30). Paul placed sexual sin at the beginning of his lists of moral prohibitions (Rom. 13:13; 1 Cor. 6:9–10; Gal. 5:19–21; Col. 3:5–8). And the last chapter of the Book of Revelation, which is the last book of the Bible, tells us that the sexually immoral will not enter God's eternal city (Rev. 22:14–15).

Every generation has faced sexual temptation and engaged in sexual sin, and there is nothing new about it. What is new is the technology that makes sexual temptation ubiquitous—and by *ubiquitous* I mean anywhere, anytime, with almost anyone, doing virtually anything. It's all there, fully accessible, and only one click (or tap) away. No generation in history has ever had to deal with sexual temptation at this level. It is nothing less than the sexual seduction of America (and the nations).

Just consider how this generation has been flooded with porn:

- "Porn sites receive more regular traffic than Netflix, Amazon, and Twitter combined each month."

- "35% of all internet downloads are porn-related."

- "34% of internet users have been exposed to unwanted porn via ads, pop-ups, etc."

- "People who admit to having extramarital affairs were over 300% more likely to admit consuming porn than those who have never had an affair."

- "At least 30% of all data transferred across the internet is porn-related."[1]

To put this in context, in December 2017 it was reported that an average of 197 million users visited Amazon.com and 127 million visited Walmart.com each month.[2] Yet a leading pornography site draws *125 million visitors per day*, with roughly *5 million adult videos* uploaded to the site in 2018 alone—enough for *115 years* of continual viewing. This is an epidemic of porn.

Back in 1953 when Hugh Hefner published the first edition of *Playboy* with a naked picture of Marilyn Monroe, there was outrage from conservative America. How scandalous! Today there are countless millions of such pictures available for instant viewing, and many of them are far are more scandalous than the original *Playboy* image. Today many a child's cell phone carries sexually suggestive pictures that would have likely made Monroe herself blush.

According to a 2015 article on the website for Exodus Cry, an organization that works to combat human trafficking, "In 1991 there were fewer than *ninety different pornographic magazines* published in America. By 1997 there were about *900 pornographic sites* on the internet. In 2011 the internet filtering software Cyber Sitter blocked *2.5 million pornographic websites*. By now [meaning 2015] that number has increased exponentially."[3] Just think of an *exponential* increase from 2.5 million. The numbers are beyond staggering—and that's just thinking about the numbers. What about the content?

Today there are chat rooms with performers stripping or engaging in sexual acts at your personal request. Many of the performers are barely even in their teens and work from their own homes to make some extra money. This is illegal for these minors and those who exploit them.

Today there are countless websites catering to every sexual fetish, bondage, and perversion.

Today even middle schoolers exchange naked pictures as they engage in sexting. The practice is illegal, as it is typically considered a form of child pornography, but it is so pervasive that many of these kids don't even realize they're breaking the law.

You don't have to subscribe to a pornographic magazine. You don't have to go to a seedy part of your city to find a porn theater. All you need is a computer. Or tablet. Or cell phone. And within seconds you have access to more sexual material than all previous generations combined.

And this is not just something teenagers and adults are confronted with. As one parenting website reports:

> According to recent data, 90% of young men age 18 have been exposed to pornography—much of which is hard-core (meaning it often involves violence and overtly explicit imagery). Of the 90%, *the average age these young men were sexualized by pornography was between 8–11 years old.* Similarly, 60% of young women by the age of 18 have been exposed to porn as well. Almost 80% of this exposure, which isn't always voluntary, is happening in the perceived safety of their homes.[4]

There are even articles today on subjects such as "The Detrimental Effects of Pornography on Small Children."[5] Small children! And there's the larger destructive effect of pornography on the family, as divorce lawyers and others have indicated that porn plays a role in around 60 percent of divorces.[6] What a deadly, often unnoticed, side effect.

But it's not just pornography that we're battling. It's the hypersexualization of our culture. You can hardly go to a news website or a sports website without seeing racy pictures. You can hardly go to a checkout counter in a store without being exposed to almost naked photos. You can hardly open your emails without sexual invitations popping up in your junk folder.

And modesty is all but gone. Every part of the body must be shown. Flesh must be displayed. Almost nothing can be hidden or covered. After all, sex sells!

Women must look perfect, enhanced by plastic surgery from buttocks to bosoms. Men must be chiseled, with six-pack abs and bulging muscles. And then clothes must be removed to leave the absolute minimum necessary (perhaps just a patch here or a strap there, and that's about it). Show off the human body, sexualize everything about the human body, and display it all for the world to see.

ESPN The Magazine even has an annual "body issue," featuring famous athletes posing nude or semi-nude, with only a camera angle (or piece of sports equipment) preserving any of their modesty. Launched in 2009, this was ESPN's answer to the annual *Sports Illustrated Swimsuit Issue*, which now leaves very little to the imagination. It's a small step from this to magazine covers featuring full nudity, and it's clearly the direction in which we're heading. (This has been common in much of Europe for years.)

Marriage has also lost its sanctity. Not only has no-fault divorce been rampant for the last generation, but living together out of wedlock has become as American as apple pie, along with having kids out of wedlock. There's nothing unusual about it! In fact, "since 1970, out-of-wedlock birth rates have soared. In 1965, 24 percent of black infants and 3.1 percent of white infants were born to single mothers. By 1990 the rates had risen to 64 percent for black infants, 18 percent for whites."[7] And 1990 seems like the good old days in comparison with today.

In 2014 the Census Bureau reported that among those for whom it had been less than five years since the birth of their first child, roughly 52 percent were married when their first child was born, 26 percent were unmarried but cohabiting with their partner, and 23 percent were neither married nor living with a partner.[8] In other words, almost 50 percent of first-born babies are born out of wedlock across our nation. Just a generation ago, a figure like this would have been unthinkable.

And there are other consequences as well. As noted by a government website, "Adolescents ages 15–24 account for nearly half of the 20 million new cases of STDs each year. Today, two in five sexually active teen girls have had an STD that can cause infertility and even death. Also, though rates of HIV are very low among adolescents, males make up more than 80 percent of HIV diagnoses among 13- to 19-year-olds."[9]

Even adultery has taken on a new twist, with websites offering married individuals illicit affairs with the person of their choice, be the affair heterosexual or homosexual. Leading the way in this is the Ashley Madison website, which came under intense scrutiny in 2015 when the names of many of its users were hacked and then leaked to the public. There were some surprising names on the list!

But how many people actually subscribe to this adulterous hookup service? In 2017, an Ashley Madison spokesman told the *New York Post* that they were signing up upwards of four hundred thousand *new users* per month. The spokesman also claimed that since Ashley Madison was founded fifteen years ago (as of 2017), the company had "signed up a total of 52.7 million users."[10]

That means there are tens of millions of people actively pursuing adultery. Tens of millions considering the possibility of an affair. Tens of millions willing to risk destroying their marriage in order to have a fling. And they are paying a company for this opportunity. Talk about a spirit of seduction. Talk about Jezebel at work. Even prostitution is glorified these days, with HBO featuring a reality TV show filmed in a Nevada brothel. Being a hooker is cool!

And speaking of HBO—which has also featured original TV shows glorifying stripteasing, sex-charged taxicab confessions, and porn stars—the company made this surprising announcement August 28, 2018. As posted on TheWrap, "'Over the past several years HBO has been winding down its late-night adult fare,' an HBO representative told TheWrap. 'While we're greatly ramping up our other original program offerings, there hasn't been a strong demand for this kind of adult programming, perhaps because it's easily available elsewhere.'"[11] Those last six words say it all. "We're dropping the adult programming 'perhaps because it's easily available elsewhere.' Why pay money for it when you can view it for free whenever you like?"

Even pimping is considered cool in these days of sexual anarchy. As Dr. Mellissa Withers noted in *Psychology Today*:

> The MTV show *Pimp My Ride* enhanced cars with painted flames, installed TVs and mini-fridges, and

leather massage seats. *Pimp My Gun* is [an] online game with a similar premise. Jay-Z made the song called "Big Pimpin" famous in a whole generation of young people (and now says he regrets it). The song "It's Hard Out Here for a Pimp," from the 2005 movie *Hustle & Flow*, which told the story of a Memphis pimp played by Terrence Howard, won the Academy Award for Best Original Song. Other artists such as 50 Cent, Nelly, and Snoop Dogg have also romanticized this industry in their song lyrics.[12]

And as if all this wasn't enough, there are now even "sexbots"—full-sized, human-looking robots with whom you can have sex. There are even sex-robot brothels. What's coming next? Or maybe the more relevant question is, What is already here?

How about this? The Office of Juvenile Justice and Delinquency Prevention, part of the US Department of Justice, reports that "juvenile sex offenders comprise more than one-quarter (25.8 percent) of all sex offenders."[13] As John Stonestreet and Anne Morse write:

> Reporters at Kansas City television station KSHB recently interviewed doctors and nurses at Children's Mercy Hospital. This is a hospital that sees 1,000 children each year who have been sexually assaulted. Heidi Olson, a nurse there who treats these victims, said she was shocked at what the data has told them: "almost half of our perpetrators are minors" between the ages of eleven and fifteen. You heard that right. We have an epidemic now of children abusing children.[14]

Yes, children are sexually abusing children, and often it is the direct result of these children acting out porn they have seen.

THE SCOURGE OF HUMAN TRAFFICKING

All this is horrific beyond words, but I've not said a word yet about the epidemic of human trafficking. Things get darker still.

It is estimated that worldwide roughly one million children are sold into sex slavery or forced labor every year, including *forty thousand per year* in America, which amounts to *109 children per day*.[15] As one website points out, "The average class in the US is 21.2 children for public elementary schools."[16] This means that each day in the United States the equivalent of five classes of elementary school students disappears. What makes this even worse is that these estimates may be low. The sexual exploitation of children is surely one of the vilest sins on the planet.

The National Center for Missing and Exploited Children has reviewed more than 267 million images of children and now averages over 25 million images annually. That equates to 480,769 images per week.[17] Yes, every single week this monitoring organization reviews almost half a million pictures of children being exploited in some manner. And this overwhelming number just represents the pictures they are able to find. How much more is hidden?

But it gets worse. As explained in a 2013 article, "A staggering statistic in [a recent university] report stated that peer to peer (P2P) users (those who share images) were more likely to have images of very young children and violent images. Of P2P users arrested in 2009, 33 percent had photos of children age three or younger and 42 percent had images of children that showed sexual violence."[18]

This is so sickening, so disturbing, and so troubling that it is amazing that God has not vomited out the entire nation, that He has not sent down fire from heaven, that He has not wiped us out once and for all. Who can imagine such evil, let alone perpetrate it? Who can conceive of kidnapping little children— even toddlers and infants—then selling them into sex slavery, where they are forced into violent sexual acts for the gratification of adult viewers? And whenever a child-porn ring is discovered, the perpetrators often turn out to be the seemingly normal people next door—your local dentist or school teacher or computer programmer or banker or blue-collar worker. The neighbors, rightly so, are shocked.

THE PLAGUE OF PORNOGRAPHY

When Hugh Hefner died in 2017, I wrote an article titled "The Death of Hugh Hefner and the End of the Sexual Revolution."[19] I was not making a prophetic declaration that his death marked the end of this disastrous era. I was expressing a fervent hope.

In the article I noted that:

- Eight-year-olds are being exposed to hard-core pornography.

- Children as young as ten are learning [in their schools!] the relative health risks of anal vs. oral vs. vaginal intercourse.

- Thirteen-year-olds are sexting each other, sometimes committing suicide when their naked pictures circulate through their school.

- Condoms have been made available to first graders. (What, pray tell, does a six-year-old child do with a condom?)

- Healthy men in their twenties cannot perform without Viagra because of their porn addictions.

- Married couples in their twenties no longer have sex because it has become so meaningless to them.

And this is not just an American problem. Gary Wilson, author of *Your Brain on Porn*, pointed to a study titled "Young Australians' Use of Pornography and Associations With Sexual Risk Behaviours." The study "reported that 100% of the young men (ages 15 to 29) have viewed porn, and 82% of the young women. Also, the age of first viewing has continued to drop, with 69% of males and 23% of females first viewing porn at age 13 or younger."[20]

What effect is this having on an entire generation of young people? How will this impact the health of their future relationships? And who knows how much more exposure they will have to porn in the days ahead.

Wilson notes that "a 2008 study reported that 14.4 percent of boys were exposed to porn prior to age 13....By the time stats were gathered in 2011, early exposure had jumped to 48.7 percent....In 2017, 39 percent of males and 4 percent of females (age 15–29) view daily, often on their smartphones."[21] What will statistics look like in 2020 and beyond?

In 2015 *Playboy* announced that it would no longer carry nude pictures in its magazine or on its website beginning in March 2016. The decision was later reversed. But *Playboy* did not temporarily abandon nude pictorials because society had become more moral; it was abandoning these pictorials because society had become so immoral that *Playboy*'s relatively mild pornography was no longer a draw.

Pornography of the most sordid kind is freely available everywhere, so who needs pictures of nude women in *Playboy*? Porn is now ubiquitous.[22] The spirit of Jezebel is thriving!

Jesus said that the false prophetess He called Jezebel "seduce[s] My servants to commit sexual immorality" (Rev. 2:20). Jehu spoke of her "harlotries" (2 Kings 9:22), and an old Jewish tradition even claimed that "Ahab was frigid by nature [passionless], so Jezebel painted pictures of two harlots on his chariot, that he might look upon them and become heated."[23]

The plague of Jezebel is upon us. And it is always connected to idolatry.

Look for a moment at the Lord's words to the church of Pergamum: "You have there those who hold the teaching of Balaam, who taught Balak to cast a stumbling block before the children of Israel, to eat things sacrificed to idols and to commit sexual immorality" (Rev. 2:14). Then look at these almost identical words spoken to the church of Thyatira: "You permit that woman Jezebel, who calls herself a prophetess, to teach and seduce My servants to commit sexual immorality and eat food sacrificed to idols" (Rev. 2:20).

Now look at this tragic indictment of King Solomon, who had been the wisest man who ever lived. (Don't skip over this passage. Read every word carefully.)

> But King Solomon loved many foreign women in addition to the daughter of Pharaoh, women of the Moabites, Ammonites, Edomites, Sidonians, and Hittites, from the nations which the LORD warned the children of Israel about, saying, "You shall not go

in to them, nor shall they come in to you, for they will surely turn your heart away toward their gods." Solomon clung to these in love. He had seven hundred wives who were princesses and three hundred concubines, and his wives turned his heart away. For when Solomon was old, his wives turned his heart away after other gods, and his heart was not perfect with the LORD his God as the heart of David his father had been. For Solomon went after Ashtoreth, the goddess of the Sidonians, and after Molek, the abomination of the Ammonites. Solomon did what was evil in the sight of the LORD and did not fully follow the LORD as his father David had done.

Then Solomon built a high place for Chemosh, the abomination of Moab, in the hill that is close to Jerusalem, and for Molek, the abomination of the children of Ammon. He did the same for all his foreign wives, who burned incense and sacrificed to their gods.

—1 KINGS 11:1–8

Idolatry and immorality are joined at the hip. And as America has become increasingly idolatrous, worshipping many gods other than Yahweh, our nation has plunged headlong into sexual immorality. We are a "free" people who are increasingly enslaved. In fact, studies now indicate that just as with other addictions, such as gambling addictions and food addictions, porn addiction causes the brain to be rewired.[24] That means that the porn addict is literally dancing to the beat of another drummer. It is a drummer who torments and drives victims deeper into bondage. It is a heartless, merciless drummer.

But porn is not only addicting. It is also degrading, especially for women who, more often than not, are the porn performers. It reduces them to physical commodities, sexual objects to be used (or abused) by an almost infinite number of strangers, and females without personality or character or depth. They are bodies that arouse and nothing more, with their images stored forever on the internet, even if they've had a change of heart.

As for the men who feed on porn (although, to be sure, an increasing number of women do as well), it actually reduces their manhood. They too become one-dimensional, viewing women through the narrow lens of sexual attraction, having a hard time entering into deep relationships, and even having difficulty performing in bed. To quote Gary Wilson again, "With respect to porn-induced sexual problems there are now 23 studies linking porn use and porn addiction to sexual problems and lower arousal to sexual stimuli....In addition, more than 50 studies now link porn use to less sexual and relationship satisfaction. Similarly, some 40 studies link porn use to poorer cognitive function and mental health problems."[25]

The Covenant Eyes website points out that "according to numerous studies, prolonged exposure to pornography leads to:

- a diminished trust between intimate couples
- the belief that promiscuity is the natural state
- cynicism about love or the need for affection between sexual partners
- the belief that marriage is sexually confining
- a lack of attraction to family and child-raising"[26]

In the end porn makes women less womanly and men less manly since there is far more to being a woman and being a man than having sex. Porn even makes us less human, reducing us to animal status, living only to fulfill our lusts. And to those with sensitive consciences, porn brings shame, self-hatred, depression, and more. The risk is surely not worth the reward, the pleasure surely not worth the penalty.

Unfortunately, this plague of pornography has swept through the church of America as well. Pastors struggle with it. Young and old battle with it. Men and women wrestle with it. Porn is knocking, even pounding, at our digital doorways day and night.

As believers we are not immune to sexual temptation, and you can be sure the spirit of Jezebel would like nothing more than to target followers of Jesus, especially leaders. We really do need to be on our guard. We have been marked by hell for destruction.

Chapter 11 of this book is devoted to practical strategies to defeat the Jezebelian stronghold in our personal lives, but for the moment, recognize this: The same devil who inspires evil men to kidnap a toddler and then rape that child on-screen is the same devil who is trying to seduce you into sexual sin. The same demonic powers that stirred Jezebel to kill God's prophets—to cut them down in cold blood— are the same demonic powers urging you to go ahead and commit adultery.

The fact is that Satan hates you. He despises you. He loathes you. He who laughed with glee as the Nazis threw living babies into fiery pits is the same one who will laugh at you as your body rots from a sexually transmitted disease or your spouse files divorce papers because of your uncontrollable porn addiction.

The last thing you want to do is give him an inch in your life. He may come to you through the seducing smile of Jezebel, but do not be deceived. Behind that smile there are sharpened fangs. Jezebel plays to kill.

CHAPTER 5

JEZEBEL AND THE SPIRIT OF BABY KILLING

THERE ARE WOMEN who have agonized over the decision to abort their baby, and years later they still feel grief and regret. What they did was wrong, but perhaps they felt trapped, as if they had no choice.

This would be like the girl who was raped by her boyfriend at the age of fifteen and couldn't live with the thought of her parents finding out about the assault or the pregnancy. Or the young mother of three little children, all by different men, who couldn't imagine bringing another child into such a chaotic world, as she had been left to herself to raise them all. Or the woman whose husband was now sick and, their finances gone, could not afford another mouth to feed. Or the mother who received the devastating news that her baby had a serious defect, because of which the child would live outside the womb a few months at best and in terrible agony every day.

These are some of the reasons women (and men) choose abortion, and we need to reach out to them with compassion, offering them forgiveness, hope, and restoration through the cross. I am *not* focusing on them in this chapter.

I *am* focusing on the women who scream for their "right" to abort their babies. I *am* focusing on those who view the child in the womb as an intrusion, a tumor to be removed, a clump of cells to be expelled. I *am* focusing on those for whom abortion is a convenient method to dispose of the results of a one-night stand, on those who have imbibed a baby-killing spirit. As expressed by proabortion feminist Florence Thomas (speaking of her abortion in France in the mid-1960s), she felt "a relief. An immense relief. This tumor went away, disappeared. I could go back to living."[1]

This, too, is the spirit of Jezebel. And while God loves these women and offers them forgiveness in Jesus, they must turn from their sinful ways and repent. They are hardening their hearts against the Lord.

Let's go back to ancient times, when idol worshippers sacrificed their babies on the altars of pagan gods. What exactly did this look like? What was their method of murder?

Jewish tradition preserves this description of babies sacrificed to Molech (sometimes called Moloch). Reading it may break your heart. Molech, we are told, "was made of brass; and they heated him from his lower parts; and his hands being stretched out, and made hot, they put the child between his hands, and it was burnt; when it vehemently cried out; but the priests beat a drum, that the father might not hear the voice of his son, and his heart might not be moved."[2] This really happened! And it happened over and over again through Israel's history.

Another Jewish tradition claims that the idol "was a hollow statue, which contained seven apartments: in one there was offered to the god, flour; turtle-doves were sacrificed in the second; sheep in the third; rams in the fourth; cakes in the fifth, and bulls in the sixth; as to the seventh cell, it was opened when they were going to sacrifice children."[3]

A Greek source dating back to the time of Alexander the Great describes the practice in Carthage, which today is the city of Tunis in Tunisia, before it fell in 146 BC:

> There stands in their midst a bronze statue of Kronos, its hands extended over a bronze brazier, the flames of which engulf the child. When the flames fall upon the body, the limbs contract and the open mouth seems almost to be laughing, until the contracted [body] slips quietly into the brazier. Thus it is that the "grin" is known as "sardonic laughter," since they die laughing.[4]

According to Greek historian Diodorus Siculus, who wrote in the first century BC, "There was in their city a bronze image of Cronus extending its hands, palms up and sloping toward the ground, so that each of the children when placed thereon rolled down and fell into a sort of gaping pit filled with fire."[5]

The horrific picture of ancient child sacrifice is painted by John Milton in his 1667 epic poem *Paradise Lost*:

> First Moloch, horrid King besmear'd with blood
> Of human sacrifice, and parents tears,
> Though for the noyse of Drums and Timbrels loud
> Thir children's cries unheard, that past through fire
> To his grim Idol.... [6]

Writing on a pro-life website, Rachel Cox uses this example to open the eyes of people who "don't think the unborn baby is a person." She suggests:

> Let's pretend a fetus is a non-human animal. Now that it's settled, allow me [to] use an example to demonstrate why killing a non-human animal in a similar fashion as one used in a human abortion is still deplorable.
>
> Let's say I have a puppy but I can't afford one at this stage in my life (lack of money is a common reason for wanting to abort). What do I do with this puppy?
>
> Since it's still small, I'm going to cram it in a blender while conscious and liquefy it to a bloody soup, disposing of the concoction in the trash.
>
> That might work for a small puppy, but what about an older dog? It won't fit in a blender.
>
> How about this then: Without using anesthesia, I'm going to chop each of the dog's legs off, one by one,

with a pair of bolt cutters. But the dog is still alive at this point, so the job isn't over yet. Now, I'm going to pick up a giant rock, slam it down on the dog's head to crush it, and then throw the dog's mangled body in a bio hazard bag.

Do you think the methods of getting rid of the dog were disturbing? Who wouldn't?[7]

Unfortunately, she explains, "those two methods are basically the same used to kill thousands of fetuses every day. Sound familiar? The first procedure I described was very similar to an aspiration abortion, commonly performed in the first trimester of pregnancy."[8] (Cox provides a clearly-illustrated diagram to make her point.)

"The second method I described," she writes, "was akin to a 'dilation and evacuation' abortion used in the second trimester" (again, backed by a diagram to prove her point). And, she notes, "There are other methods of abortion besides these. Not one of them could be described as non-violent, and they all obviously result in death."[9]

Yet we have aborted nearly *61 million babies* since 1973,[10] almost equal to the combined populations of Peru and Venezuela and more than the population of England, and all by violent means. What kind of wickedness is this?

Yet for many Americans this is a hidden sin, something done behind closed doors in a "women's health clinic" or the like, out of sight and out of mind. As expressed by pro-life leader Eric Scheidler:

I think it's extremely pleasing to the devil when an abortion takes place....This wickedness happens in the dark. The womb is an invisible place. We don't see the abortion happening. Even those photographs we have [of aborted babies] are very rare. They are hard to come by. This is a hidden evil. It's one that digs its roots so deeply in our society because it happens in secret, and so many people are complicit in it, and it gradually wears away people's sensitivity.[11]

And as our hearts get harder and harder, we have fewer and fewer problems with even the most extreme forms of abortion, particularly late-term abortions. That's why, when New York passed its radical, proabortion law in early 2019, allowing abortions up to the moment before delivery if desired, the legislators cheered and One World Trade Center was lit up in pink.[12]

What exactly happens during this brutal, late-term procedure? Basing his description on a mother's firsthand account of what it felt like to abort her baby while eight months pregnant, Jonathon van Maren provides this grisly summary:

> This the reality of late-term abortion: An abortionist sweating with the effort of crushing a nearly full-term baby's skull and tear[ing] his body to pieces, before dropping those pieces on a tray so that a nurse can piece him back together to make sure nothing got left behind. And then, the doctors can place their fresh kill in a coffin so that the little boy's shattered corpse can be given the respect he was denied in life.[13]

Or consider this firsthand testimony from Brenda Pratt Shafer, a registered nurse from Dayton, Ohio, who testified before the House Judiciary Committee on March 21, 1996, about a partial-birth abortion she witnessed on a pre-born baby boy at six months gestation.

He delivered the baby's body and the arms—everything but the head. The doctor kept the baby's head just inside the uterus. The baby's little fingers were clasping and unclasping, and his feet were kicking. Then the doctor stuck the scissors through the back of his head, and the baby's arms jerked out in a flinch, a startle reaction, like a baby does when he thinks that he might fall. The doctor opened up the scissors, stuck a high-powered suction tube into the opening and sucked the baby's brains out. Now the baby was completely limp.[14]

What happened next?

[The doctor] delivered the baby's head. He cut the umbilical cord and delivered the placenta. He threw that baby in a pan, along with the placenta and the instruments he'd used. I saw the baby move in the pan. I asked another nurse and she said it was just "reflexes." I have been a nurse for a long time and I have seen a lot of death—people maimed in auto accidents, gunshot wounds, you name it. I have seen surgical procedures of every sort. But in all my professional years, I had never witnessed anything like this.[15]

So, a doctor delivers the body and arms of a living baby, sticks scissors through the back of his or her head, and sucks out the baby's brains. Then, with the skull collapsed, the doctor delivers the rest of the now-motionless child.

Is this any better than burning babies on the altar of Moloch? How would John Milton describe it? Yet in today's culture, comedians can joke about abortion and activists can celebrate it.

Speaking at a White House correspondents' dinner in 2018, comedian Michelle Wolf said Vice President Pence "is also very anti-choice. He thinks abortion is murder, which, first of all, don't knock it till you try it. And when you do try it, really knock it. You know, you got to get that baby out of there. And yeah, sure, you can groan all you want. I know a lot of you are very anti-abortion, you know, unless it's the one you got for your secret mistress."[16]

Oh, how funny! Yes, be sure to really knock that baby out of there!

AMERICA'S FIRST FEMINISTS WERE PRO-LIFE

In contrast with today's radical-feminist, baby-killing spirit, the women's movement in America in the late 1800s was anything but proabortion. Two of the pioneer leaders, Victoria Woodhull and Tennessee Claflin, said this:

> We are aware that many women attempt to excuse themselves for procuring abortions, upon the ground that it is not murder. But the fact of resort to so weak an argument only shows the more palpably that they fully realize the enormity of the crime. Is it not equally destroying the would-be future oak to crush the sprout before it pushes its head above the sod, as to cut down the sapling, or to saw down the tree? Is it not equally to destroy life, to crush it in the very germ, and to take it when the germ has evolved to any given point in the line of its development?[17]

In the words of Susan B. Anthony:

Guilty? Yes. No matter what the motive, love of ease, or a desire to save from suffering the unborn innocent, the woman is awfully guilty who commits the deed. It will burden her conscience in life, it will burden her soul in death; but oh!, thrice guilty is he who, for selfish gratification, heedless of her prayers, indifferent to her fate, drove her to the desperation which impelled her to the crime.[18]

Nineteenth century suffragist Sarah F. Norton wrote:

Child murderers practice their profession without let or hindrance, and open infant butcheries un-questioned...Is there no remedy for all this ante-natal child murder?...Perhaps there will come a time when...an unmarried mother will not be despised because of her motherhood...and when the right of the unborn to be born will not be denied or interfered with.[19]

These women minced no words, referring to abortionists as "child murderers," with well-known suffragist Elizabeth Cady Stanton classifying abortion as "infanticide."[20] And these were the radical leaders of the early women's movement in America!

Contrast their sentiments with those of proabortion leaders and their allies today. For example, a 2015 article featuring "The 25 All-Time Greatest Pro-Choice Quotes" offers gems like these:[21]

Listen to the pregnant woman. Value her. She values the life growing inside her. Listen to the pregnant woman, and you cannot help but defend her right to abortion.

—AYELET WALDMAN

But do *not* under any circumstances listen to the baby in that pregnant woman's womb.

My argument has always been that nature has a master plan pushing every species toward procreation and that it is our right and even obligation as rational human beings to defy nature's fascism. Nature herself is a mass murderer, making casual, cruel experiments and condemning 10,000 to die so that one more fit will live and thrive.

—CAMILLE PAGLIA, PROFESSOR AND SOCIAL CRITIC

So if nature is a mass murderer, we should join the murder party. It's survival of the fittest, after all!

After listening to Rick Santorum, I'm now for late-term abortions (say up to age 53).

—QUENTIN R. BUFOGLE, WRITER

Recall what we just read about late-term abortions and ask yourself: What human being with a real conscience would make a joke about late-term abortions?

SHOUT YOUR ABORTION

For the proabortion camp, though, abortion is no big deal at all. In the foreword to a book edited by her Shout Your Abortion movement cofounder Amelia Bonow, Lindy West wrote, "Abortion is normal. Abortion is common. Abortion is happening. Abortion is a necessary medical procedure. Abortion makes people's lives better. Abortion needs to be legal, safe, and accessible to everyone. Abortion is a thing you can say out loud."[22]

And how did Bonow explain this "necessary medical procedure" to two young girls in a "Kids Meet" video?

> You go to the doctor, and they put this little straw inside of your cervix, and then inside of your uterus, and then they just suck the pregnancy out. And it was like a crappy dentist appointment or something. It was just like...'This is a body thing that's kind of uncomfortable,' but then it was over, and I felt really just grateful that I wasn't pregnant anymore.[23]

Yes, abortion is just another medical procedure, no different than removing a cancerous growth or getting an appendectomy or going to the dentist. No big deal. Nothing to do with morality. Just like dealing with a bad appendix. Or a bad tooth. Get rid of that unnecessary thing and toss it away. Done! And Bonow wanted the kids to know that it's "all part of God's plan."[24]

Indeed, Bonow, West, and their abortion-shouting colleagues want us to know that "Abortion is freedom.... Without abortion we are not free."[25]

And, to repeat, they claim it is not a big deal at all. As Bonow explains, "Abortion has been a normal part of reproductive life since the beginning of time. Why wouldn't it be? It's easy to get pregnant, it's very difficult to raise a baby, and terminating a pregnancy is generally not risky or complicated."[26] By this logic, we could say: "It's very easy to get pregnant and have kids but very difficult to deal with a toddler experiencing the terrible twos. Killing them is generally not risky or complicated." Or perhaps this same logic could be applied to rebellious teens? Getting rid of them, to be sure, would be a lot more difficult, but hey, with some creativity, it could be done.

I hope you find it as repulsive to read these words as I found it to write them. And I hope you realize that it is just as much an assault on innocent life to slice up a baby in the womb as it is to slice up a child outside the womb. Little wonder, then, that the proabortion camp is now talking about justification for infanticide.[27] Why not?

As for the alleged therapeutic wonders of abortion, it looks like the Shout Your Abortion crowd failed to consider the millions of women who had abortions and have lived with pain and regret ever since. In fact, some of the most unforgettable, gut-wrenching calls I have ever received in the history of my radio broadcast have been from listeners who had abortions in years past. Women have called in and broken down sobbing while recounting abortions they had thirty or even forty years ago. The memory still haunts them. Even men have called in weeping to talk about taking their girlfriends to have abortions. They know God has forgiven them, but the memory still stings.[28]

Then there was the call from an anonymous Christian woman working at Planned Parenthood but experiencing great conflict. By God's grace she never went back to her job and has an amazing story of redemption to tell. But as the manager of an abortion clinic she witnessed firsthand what happened to those mothers leaving her building minus the babies who were previously in their wombs. They were not in the shouting mood.[29]

As she explained some months after she called my show, having started a brand-new life and no longer anonymous (her name is Crystal Eldridge), "The women would cry...99% of people were not happy, and there were journals in the back room—in the recovery room—that the women were encouraged to write in, to kind of get their feelings out. And I could never read them in full because I cried too hard." These women even "planted flowers in the rose garden for the babies, and that they didn't want to have to do that [abortion], that they didn't know of any other way."[30]

Worst of all, "Crystal had nightmares about the POC room—where babies were pieced back together after abortion to make sure all their body parts were accounted for—and witnessed how women's abortions did not go as smoothly as the public is led to believe."[31] (POC stands for "products of conception," such a sterile name for such murderous results.) I don't know how anyone could hear her sobbing on the radio while talking about this without being moved.[32]

Contrast this with one of the stories in the *Shout Your Abortion* book, where a budding comedian, El Sanchez, hears some surprising words from the abortion doctor in the recovery room after the procedure. It was the doctor's custom to give flowers to her last patient each day, but she surprised El with flowers, saying, "I know you're not the last patient, but you're getting these flowers because you're the funniest abortion I've ever performed." And what does El have to say about this now? "She hands me the flowers, and the story of the greatest achievement of my comedy career."[33]

Yes, the funniest abortion ever! Absolutely hysterical! A true comedic triumph! Don't just shout your abortion. Laugh about it!

JEZEBEL IS OBSESSED

But Jezebel is aggressive. She is obsessed. She is determined. "I must have my right to abort!" Abortion is considered a matter of "reproductive justice."[34]

During the hearing to confirm Brett Kavanaugh to the Supreme Court, I was reminded of the famous line that "hell hath no fury like a woman scorned." This prompted me to write an article titled "Prepare for the Wrath of the Pro-Abortion Militants," which ended by saying "that hell hath no fury like that of the militant pro-abortionists."[35]

The same day my piece was published, on the very same website Jennifer Hartline posted a similarly themed article that was shared more than one hundred thousand times. Hers was titled "It's Not Kavanaugh. It's Roe," and her article ended with these words: "They hate Kavanaugh because they love abortion and he does not. Hell hath no fury like 'women's rights' scorned."[36] Was there a message the Spirit was speaking?

Referring to the pitched opposition to Kavanaugh's confirmation, Hartline wrote, "This is about abortion. It's about the larger sexual ideology as well, but abortion first and foremost. This is about nothing more than demolishing a candidate for the Supreme Court whom they did not choose, and who poses a serious threat to their golden idol. Abortion is both sacrament and god."[37] She was absolutely right. Just as child sacrifice was directly tied to idolatry, so too abortion itself is an idol, a "sacrament and god."

She continued:

> A country that shrugs off the evidence of what abortion really is and chants all the louder about "freedom" and "equality" can never claim to achieve either. *Roe*

v. Wade is the litmus test to end all litmus tests. That's because abortion is the moral "issue" to end all issues. It is uniquely defining of a culture and an individual. People who support the act of butchering the most defenseless and innocent of all human beings, blithely calling it "choice" can hardly plant their flag on a civilized hill.

A nation that considers killing its own children to be the *pièce de résistance* of its fight for empowerment and justice is suffering a suicidal delusion.[38]

And then these piercing and prophetic words:

And that's precisely what we've got here in America. The delusion is so hypnotic and addictive that nothing must be permitted to question it or come against it. There *must* be sexual pleasure without price. *Nothing* matters more than sexual gratification. The god of the groin is perpetually unsatisfied and greedy.

So the modern sophisticated pagans want to continue exposing the unwanted child to birds of prey on a rock in the midday sun. The allegiance they require to abortion-on-demand is no different and no better. Except that today they remove those lucrative brains and organs first. (I guess our ancestors didn't know there was money to be made from baby body parts.)

After 45 years of this demonic delusion, with millions of babies picked apart by vultures in lab coats, along comes the possibility that finally the most sickening injustice of all time may be undone, and the pelvic Left is twelve different kinds of hysterical.[39]

Sexual immorality, idolatry, abortion—a threefold cord that is not easily broken. It is as old as Jezebel and even older. And it brought Israel under the wrath of God. As the psalmist declared:

> They did not destroy the nations as the LORD commanded them, but they mixed among the nations and learned their deeds; they served their idols, which were a snare to them. Yes, they sacrificed their sons and their daughters to demons, and poured out innocent blood, even the blood of their sons and of their daughters, whom they sacrificed to the idols of Canaan, and the land was polluted with blood. Thus were they defiled by their acts and acted like whores with these actions. Therefore the wrath of the LORD was kindled against His people, and He abhorred His own inheritance.
>
> —PSALM 106:34–40

How close is our nation to experiencing the fury of God's wrath? To ignore that question is to bury our heads in the sand. America is teetering ever closer to collapse.

The good news is that more and more Americans are waking up to the evil of abortion, including abortion providers, from doctors to nurses to security guards. And many women who had abortions have become pro-life champions. The bad news is that abortion on demand could be largely eradicated from our land if God's people simply got involved. As theologian Francis Schaeffer reportedly put it, "Every abortion clinic should have a sign in front of it saying, 'Open by the permission of the church.'"[40] How these words cut to the heart!

He also said that "certainly every Christian ought to be praying and working to nullify the abominable abortion law. But as we work and pray, we should have in mind not only this important issue as though it stood alone. Rather, we should be struggling and praying that this whole other total entity—the material-energy, chance world view—can be rolled back with all its results across all of life."[41]

What then can we do? We should first repent for our corporate hardness and indifference.[42] Then we should get involved however we can—from praying to supporting pro-life clinics to sharing the gospel in front of abortion mills to running for office to voting for pro-life candidates to adopting unwanted babies and more. And we should offer God's mercy to all those guilty of the sin of abortion. The blood of Jesus can cleanse this ugly stain too.

But let us not lose sight of the urgency of the hour and the magnitude of our sin. Our heavenly Father hears the silent cries of these slaughtered little ones, and as their sliced-up, burned-up, and torn-up body parts pile up in trash bins (or, worse still, are sold for profit[43]), their blood shouts aloud to heaven. As we cast our glance around the world, the cry of their blood is constant and penetrating and unrelenting. Yes, "abortion was the number one cause of death worldwide in 2018, with more than 41 million children killed before birth."[44]

How much longer will the Lord restrain His anger? Jezebel *must* be defeated.

CHAPTER 6

JEZEBEL AND RADICAL FEMINISM

MAKE NO MISTAKE about it: These women are mad. Very mad. Raging mad.

Their intense, bottled-up anger is expressed in the title of Rebecca Traister's best-selling book *Good and Mad: The Revolutionary Power of Women's Anger*, a book in which the word *anger* is found 332 times, *rage* 167 times, *fury* 112 times, and *wrath* 16 times.[1] (Significantly, the name Trump is found 219 times, but we'll explain the relevance of that in chapter 10.)

A poem by author and activist Alice Walker at the beginning of the book says it all. The feminine, Walker writes, is neither dead nor asleep; she is angry, seething even, and "biding her time."[2]

Now her time—the time for radical feminism—has come. And it has come with a vengeance.

Traister also quotes an anthem written by Meredith Tax to the tune of the "Battle Hymn of the Republic." Tax proclaims that her eyes have seen the glory of the fire of women's anger. No longer prisoners who can be appeased with wedding rings and no longer willing to bend when they are denied the true value of their labor, these women are angry—and they're marching on.[3]

To be clear, though, Traister's book is not a mindless screed appealing to random female rage. She is thoughtful and quite pointed in her writing. And the undeniable fact is that over the centuries, including right here in America, there have been ample causes for women's anger. As Traister explains:

> This book is about women so angry at slavery and lynching that they risked their lives and reputations and pioneered new forms of public expression for women, including speeches in front of mixed-gender

and mixed-race audiences; about women so furious at their lack of a franchise that they walked 150 miles from New York City to Albany to petition for the vote, went on hunger strikes, and picketed outside the White House. Women so angry that they stayed angry for the decades—their lifetimes—it took to get the right to vote, first via the Nineteenth Amendment and then the Voting Rights Act, their rage leading them to acts of civil disobedience—marches and sit-ins and voting when it was not legal to do so—for which they would be jailed, beaten. Women who took conversations that had historically been whispered and chose instead to broadcast them via open-air rallies and in the pages of newspapers and in lawsuits and in front of political conventions and judiciary committees.[4]

The international Me Too movement has exposed the depth of sexual abuse and harassment to which many women have been subjected, including the fact that in some countries women are routinely beaten, burned by acid, or killed for refusing their suitors or violating a family code of honor. And anywhere that a woman can do the same work a man can do, just as well as a man does it, without being equally compensated, something is not right.

Not all feminism is bad, and not all women's movements are misguided.[5] To the contrary, female activists have done much good to change the world, and there are godly women who identify as Christian feminists.[6] Jesus included women in His inner circle, and Paul spoke highly of some of his female fellow-laborers.[7]

But there is a radical feminism that is destructive. It sees marriage as an outdated, slavish institution; regards motherhood as a lesser calling; and views children as an intrusion. It is not merely pro-woman; it is also anti-man and anti-family, virulently so.

Males are downright evil (especially, these days in America, white males). The patriarchy must be overthrown. Women must reign supreme. *This too is the spirit of Jezebel.*

As expressed in a tweet by a black woman named Taiyesha Baker, who put specific focus on white males, "Every white woman raises a detriment to society when they raise a son. Someone with the HIGHEST propensity to be a terrorist, rapist, racist, killer, and domestic violence all-star. Historically every son you had should be sacrificed to the wolves."[8]

Emily Lindin, a white contributor to *Teen Vogue*, shared some similar sentiments, although in her case the hostility was not as extreme and was not limited to white males. She tweeted, "Here's an unpopular opinion: I'm actually not at all concerned about innocent men losing their jobs over false sexual assault/harassment allegations."[9] Come again? You have no problem with *innocent males* losing their jobs after being falsely accused? You wouldn't mind if it was a fine, respectable, upright, ethical, hardworking, kindhearted man whose reputation was sullied and whose career destroyed because of outright lies? You wouldn't mind if this happened to your father or your brother (or husband, if you are married)? Precisely so. As she explained, "Sorry. If some innocent men's reputations have to take a hit in the process of undoing the patriarchy, that is a price I am absolutely willing to pay."[10] Patriarchy must be crushed, and there will always be innocent casualties of war. So be it.

The sentiments of radical feminism are extreme, challenging the very fundamentals of our society. That's why some of the central issues taken on by radical feminists include:

- "A critique of motherhood, marriage, the nuclear family, and sexuality, questioning how much of our culture is based on patriarchal assumptions"

- "A critique of other institutions, including government and religion, as centered historically in patriarchal power"[11]

And just how far do these critiques go? The Thought Catalog website offers "23 Quotes From Feminists That Will Make You Rethink Feminism." (The quotes were compiled by Jake Fillis and posted on May 17, 2014, which was before the most recent spike in radical feminism, which traces back to the election of President Trump in 2016.) Some of the quotes include:[12]

I feel that "man-hating" is an honorable and viable political act, that the oppressed have a right to class-hatred against the class that is oppressing them.
　　　　　—ROBIN MORGAN, *Ms.* MAGAZINE EDITOR

The nuclear family must be destroyed...Whatever its ultimate meaning, the break-up of families now is an objectively revolutionary process.
　　　　　—LINDA GORDON, WRITER AND HISTORIAN

Marriage as an institution developed from rape as a practice.
　　　　　—ANDREA DWORKIN, WRITER

Since marriage constitutes slavery for women, it is clear that the women's movement must concentrate on attacking this institution. Freedom for women cannot be won without the abolition of marriage.

—SHEILA CRONAN, FEMINIST ACTIVIST

The proportion of men must be reduced to and maintained at approximately 10% of the human race.

—SALLY MILLER GEARHART, IN HER ESSAY
"THE FUTURE—IF THERE IS ONE—IS FEMALE"

If life is to survive on this planet, there must be a decontamination of the Earth. I think this will be accompanied by an evolutionary process that will result in a drastic reduction of the population of males.

—MARY DALY, FEMINIST PHILOSOPHER

Probably the only place where a man can feel really secure is in a maximum security prison, except for the imminent threat of release.

—GERMAINE GREER,
FEMINIST WRITER AND ACADEMIC

This is the mindset of radical feminism. And be assured that these quotes are not from unknown, unheralded feminists. Robin Morgan has been a longtime, major feminist voice, once alleging that Charles Manson was "only the logical extreme of the normal American male's fantasy."[13] Linda Gordon is a prize-winning historian.[14] Andrea Dworkin was well-known for her war against pornography.[15] Sheila Cronan was a contributor to the 1973 collection *Radical Feminism*.[16] Sally Miller Gearhart was "the first open lesbian to obtain a tenure-track faculty position when she was hired by San Francisco State University, where she helped establish one of the first women and gender study programs in the country."[17] Mary Daly, also a lesbian, taught as a philosopher and theologian at the Jesuit-run Boston College.[18] And Germaine Greer is one of the best-known feminists in the world, still active at eighty years old but famous since 1970 when her groundbreaking book *The Female Eunuch* was published.[19]

Now go back and re-read those quotes. They are not the voice of a handful of fringe extremists. They represent the sentiments of many a radical feminist. And note how they agree with the radical philosophy of the Marxist leader Leon Trotsky: "To alter the position of woman *at the root* is possible only if all the conditions of social, family, and domestic existence are altered."[20]

Not surprisingly other essays in the 1973 *Radical Feminism* collection focus on topics such as "Man-Hating," "Loving Another Woman," and "The [Expletive] Manifesto," which states:

> The most prominent characteristic of all [expletive] is that they rudely violate conceptions of proper sex role behavior. They violate them in different ways, but they all violate them....
>
> What is disturbing about a [expletive] is that she is androgynous. She incorporates within herself qualities traditionally defined as "masculine" as well as "feminine."[21]

But the spirit of radical feminism is not limited to women. In some circles *men themselves* are joining together in a battle against "toxic masculinity."[22] That's why in September 2016 Duke University launched the Duke Men's Project, hosted by the campus Women's Center and offering "a nine-week program for 'male-identified' students that discusses male privilege, patriarchy, 'the language of dominance,' rape culture, pornography, machismo and other topics."[23] (Apparently, women who identify as men were welcome but not men who identified as women.)

A student editorial supporting the project wanted to make clear that it was not some kind of "reeducation camp" devoted to the "feminization of America" (with reference to a Dennis Prager article; see chapter 7). Instead the project was something put together by men, entirely for men.[24]

Yet, the editorial continued, the project was of tremendous importance because "the weaponization of masculinity and femininity continues to broadly affect all of us."[25] And what exactly does this "weaponization" look like? According to Duke junior Dipro Bhowmik, who is on the leadership team of the Duke Men's Project, the goal is for male students to reflect critically on their own masculinity, to recognize the nature of toxic masculinity, and to "create healthier" masculinities. Or, as expressed by Alex Bressler, who is also on the leadership team, the program will help men "proactively deconstruct our masculinity."[26] Jezebel would be pleased.

LIBERAL WOMEN NEUTERING MEN?

Speaking at a conservative women's gathering in 2011, Allen West, then serving as a member of the House of Representatives from Florida, made these controversial comments, which helped earn him an entry in *The Book of Jezebel*.[27] Pointing to the ancient Greek Spartans, he said:

> We need you to come in and lock shields, and strengthen up the men who are going to the fight for you. To let these other women know on the other side—these Planned Parenthood women, the Code

Pink women, and all of these women that have been neutering American men and bringing us to the point of this incredible weakness—to let them know that we are not going to have our men become subservient. That's what we need you to do. Because if you don't, then the debt will continue to grow...deficits will continue to grow.[28]

His comments drew immediate scorn from liberal websites, including Jezebel.com, which reported:

Allen West, the Republican congressman endorsed by Sarah Palin, has asserted what women's roles in politics should be: Breeding warriors.

Anything that doesn't involve breeding is anathema, which of course includes Planned Parenthood, West announced in a recent speech before a conservative women's group in his home state of Florida.[29]

Of course, you could parse West's comments carefully and find some better ways to express things, but he really did hit a specific nail on the head. Men *are* being neutered by the baby-killing culture, and when they are complicit in aborting a child they have helped produce, they degenerate from fathers to copulaters. (To the critics who plan to quote this, have at it, but please quote this line as well: A man who will have intimate sexual relationships with a woman and not take responsibility for the consequences of his actions is *not* acting like a man.)

Really now, to father a child is to bring a child into the world and care for him or her—to become a father, not simply to have sex. Yet today not only do we have a generation of copulaters who cop out on being fathers, leaving the pregnant women to fend for themselves, but we also have a generation of anonymous sperm donors who sell their goods for profit and leave their offspring disconnected from them for life.[30] These men may not be neutered physically, but there is certainly an emotional neutering that takes place.

It's the same when men fail to take their roles as protectors and providers in deference to the spirit of radical feminism. (More on this later in this chapter.) This produces a neutering as well. Jezebel continues to emasculate men.

FATHERS ON TV

The world of popular entertainment joins right in, also emasculating men, in particular the fathers. Just think back to the early days of TV when the father was the source of wisdom, of stability, of strength; when the father was honored. Think back to shows like *Leave It to Beaver, Ozzie and Harriet, My Three Sons*, or *Father Knows Best.* (Yes, the fathers knew best!) Then contrast that esteemed, respected role of the husband and father with the beleaguered, mocked, figure of today, a figure scorned by his children and ridiculed by his wife.

Back in 2005 John Tierney published an op-ed in the *New York Times* titled "The Doofus Dad," beginning with this anecdote: One evening, after watching an episode of *The Simpsons* with his son, the six-year-old asked him, "Why are dads on TV so dumb?" Why indeed!

This prompted Tierney to ask himself where fathers have gone wrong today. He writes:

> We spend twice as much time with our kids as we
> did two decades ago, but on television we're oblivious ("Jimmy Neutron"), troubled ("The Sopranos"),

deranged ("Malcolm in the Middle") and generally incompetent ("Everybody Loves Raymond"). Even if Dad has a good job, like the star of "Home Improvement," at home he's forever making messes that must be straightened out by Mom.[31]

In fact, "a study by the National Fatherhood Initiative found that fathers are eight times more likely than mothers to be portrayed negatively on network television."[32] Does this not have a neutering effect? (And note that this study is now fourteen years old. How much worse are things today?)

Writing on February 27, 2013, Sarah Petersen observed that, "If you watch TV, then you've most likely witnessed the portrayal of the modern-day husband and father as lazy, incompetent and stupid." She continued, "Just these three characteristics are sure to bring to mind one commercial or sitcom that personifies this type of man."[33]

And what is beyond these negative caricatures of men? According to Courtney Kane, also writing in the *New York Times* in 2005:

> The portrayals began as a clever reversal of traditional gender roles in campaigns, prompted by the ire of women and feminist organizations over decades of ads using stereotyped imagery of an incompetent, bumbling housewife who needed to be told which coffee or cleanser to buy.
>
> As those images disappeared, the pendulum swung, producing campaigns portraying men in general, and husbands and fathers in particular, as objects of ridicule, pity or even scorn. Among them are ads for Bud Light, Domino's, Hummer, T-Mobile and Verizon.[34]

How fascinating. This wasn't just some random, widespread coincidence. This was quite intentional. We cannot over-estimate the impact this constant negative bombardment has on our psyches. The influence of TV is massive.

Writing on July 2, 2015, for the National Fatherhood Initiative (NFI) website, Melissa Steward cites the research of NFI President Christopher A. Brown:

> The portrayal of fathers in commercials and advertising play a huge role in how we see fathers. Studies show commercials rarely portray men as nurturers. Brown points out one study found *"when fathers were included in commercials, none of them were portrayed as nurturers whereas half of mothers were portrayed as nurturers* (Gentry & Harrison, 2010)."
>
> Brown says that fathers are still often portrayed by consumer brands as one extreme or the other. On the one side fathers are shown as incompetent, foolish, and emotionally disconnected as parents. "The double standard involves competent, wise, emotionally connected mothers who must often rescue those fathers," says Brown.[35]

This was further confirmed on Dad Blog UK, with reference to a new BBC sitcom called *Motherland*:

> The few men that appear in the show are two-dimensional. They are either camp, effeminate stay at home dads or alpha-men, uninterested in family life and found on the golf-course, stag weekends or team-building weekends with colleagues.

Motherland's portrayal of men encapsulates everything that is wrong with the media's portrayal of modern fathers. It features none of the men who I regularly see in the playground on the school run. There are no men who work from home, it features no men who work four-day weeks so they can spend a day a week with the kids or men who work shifts and do the school run when shift patterns permit.[36]

So the men in this sitcom are either feminized or hypermasculinized, either effeminate or into stag weekends. Jezebel must be smiling.

BACK TO OUR UNIVERSITIES

Turning back to our colleges and universities, the Princeton University human resources department, in an effort to be politically correct, issued a policy in 2016 "that aims to make the department more gender inclusive."[37] Yes, according to the original memo, employees must "refrain from the use of gendered language," since the gender binary of male and female "does not take into consideration individuals who identify as otherwise, including and not limited to transgender, genderqueer, gender non-conforming, and/or intersex."[38]

What, exactly, does this look like in practice? Instead of saying "average man," employees are urged to say "average person" or "ordinary person." And rather than saying "best man for the job," they should say "best person for the job," while "layman" should be replaced with "layperson" or "nonspecialist." Of course, "man and wife" have to go, being replaced by the far superior "spouses" or "partners," while "man hours" is to be replaced by "person hours" or "work hours."[39] (I can hear someone ask, "So, how many person hours will it take to complete this job?")

Naturally, "manpower" is out, to be replaced by "personnel" or "staff" or "workers" or "workforce," while even "man made [sic]" is off limits, to be replaced by "artificial, handmade, manufactured, synthetic." And God forbid you use the word "workmanlike," since that nasty m-word is hidden right there in plain sight. Instead, one should say "skillful."[40]

But it gets worse. A headline on the Weasel Zippers website (devoted to "Scouring the Bowels of the Internet") announced, "Feminist Declares the Invention of the Alphabet the Root of Sexism, Misogyny and Patriarchy..." The website cited an article called "How the Invention of the Alphabet Usurped Female Power in Society and Sparked the Rise of Patriarchy in Human Culture."[41] Quoting from Leonard Shlain's 1998 book *The Alphabet Versus the Goddess: The Conflict Between Word and Image*, we are told that "one pernicious effect of literacy has gone largely unnoticed: writing subliminally fosters a patriarchal outlook. Writing of any kind, but especially its alphabetic form, diminishes feminine values and with them, women's power in the culture."[42] How did we miss that? And to think: all the time we were learning the ABCs, we had no idea we were oppressing women in the process.

And here's something else we missed. The idea of Santa Claus being a man is antiquated and offensive! Yes, "Santa might be too antiquated for modern times, and one company has offered up the idea of a possible gender-neutral Father Christmas."[43] So a graphics company surveyed four hundred people in the US and the UK, asking for input on how best to modernize Santa. The results? "In terms of what gender Santa should be, nearly 19 percent of U.S. respondents said the patriarch of Christmas should be identified neither as male or female. More than 10 percent said a woman should fill the role."[44] After all, in 2018 (when the survey was done), are we still talking about "Father Christmas"? Seriously?

Thankfully the great majority of respondents were fine leaving Santa as is. But almost 20 percent of the respondents wanted a gender-neutral Santa. Think about *that*. (Perhaps the name could remain the same, since it's a female-sounding name, now used by a male?) And does it matter that there's a historical background to the Santa myth, going back to an actual man (yes, a dreaded male!) famed for his sacrificial generosity? I'm speaking of St. Nicholas, "the 4th-century Bishop of Myra, whose reputation for generosity and kindness—including secretly leaving gold in a poor man's home on multiple occasions—inspired tales that eventually evolved into the modern story of Santa Claus's Christmas Eve flight around the world."[45] Blot that sexist memory out!

A December 2014 article featuring "10 of the Craziest Ideas Pushed in the Name of Feminism," informs us that:

> French feminist Luce Irigaray calls "E=mc2" a "sexed equation." She claims that it is sexist because [it] "privileges the speed of light over other speeds that are vitally necessary to us." Irigaray thinks it's sexist for the formula to "privilege that which goes faster."
>
> Irigaray believes that all of physics is sexist. She sees a massive male conspiracy in physics that has made fluid mechanics, which she associates with the feminine, less developed than solid mechanics. She thinks male physicists are deliberately not studying fluid mechanics because men's bodies don't have a particular fluid in them: menstrual fluid.[46]

Complete and utter nonsense, you say? Absolute drivel, you think? I concur. But note that this woman is no intellectual or philosophical slouch. "Since 1964," the same website states, "she has been employed as a researcher at the French National Centre for Scientific Research and is currently [as of 2014] France's director of research in philosophy."[47] The Wikipedia entry describes Irigaray as "a Belgian-born French feminist, philosopher, linguist, psycholinguist, psychoanalyst and cultural theorist. She is best known for her works *Speculum of the Other Woman* (1974) and *This Sex Which Is Not One* (1977)."[48] Yet she argues that "male physicists are deliberately not studying fluid mechanics because men's bodies don't have a particular fluid in them: menstrual fluid."[49] (Note to Ms. Irigaray: Males have plenty of fluids in their bodies too, including blood, which is pretty important. They also discharge fluids through sweat and urination. But why get caught up in trivialities?)

Putting this madness aside, though, there is one thing on which all radical feminists would agree: male authority must be overthrown. That is where the real battle lies, and that is where the final battle must be fought. As long as men dominate in positions of authority and as long as men are perceived as "the head of the home," radical feminists will fight.

Here too Jezebel will cheer them on. To quote another, traditional Jewish reflection, "Four women assumed rulership in the world: Jezebel and Athaliah [assumed rulership] of Israel, Shemirmamith [wife of Nebuchadnezzar] and Vashti [assumed rulership] of the nations of the world."[50]

And this is where my words will stir up a fresh (and heated) controversy: I believe that, according to the Scriptures, *the Lord has appointed men to have the primary role in governmental authority*. That is why the vast majority of national leaders in the Bible were men, and that is why the vast majority of spiritual leaders in the Bible were men.

That does *not* mean that all men have authority over all women, nor does it mean any man has the right to hurt, abuse, or sinfully dominate another woman, be it a wife, a daughter, an employee, a parishioner, or any other. Never! And it does *not* mean men are superior to women or have a higher standing than women.

In particular, in Jesus there is neither male nor female, which does not mean the obliteration of gender and sex distinctions (see the next chapter for more about that). But it does mean males and females have equal status and equal standing in Jesus—that we are equally children of God, equally branches of the vine, equally parts of the body, equally priests to the Lord, equally filled with the Spirit, equally loved and called by the Father. (See Galatians 3:28.)

At the same time, there is a reason that Israel was led by kings, not queens; that the priests were males; and that the twelve apostles were men, not women. There is a reason Paul spoke of male overseers rather than female overseers. There is a reason we have the writings of the church fathers rather than the church mothers.

Without a doubt, where the gospel has gone over the centuries, women have been liberated and even celebrated. This has been well-documented by historians and sociologists,[51] and it's easy to compare the liberties enjoyed by women in Christian societies to those in Muslim societies. But there's no denying that God has made men and women uniquely and differently, and that females have gifts that males do not, and males have gifts that females do not.

My wife, Nancy, is the strongest person I know. (We've been best friends since 1974 and married since 1976.) When she has a conviction, she is completely immovable, seemingly impervious to outside pressure or consequences, unmoved by the fear of man. She influences me far more than I influence her, and I look to her for wisdom and advice far more than she looks to me for the same.

She has worked with architects to design a house for us and then worked with the general contractor to oversee every detail of the build, and she has done the same with major landscaping projects. She served as the director of admissions at our ministry school for years, worked as the liaison to our pastoral care department, and was our school administrator for a season.

She is a highly capable, clear-headed woman, and when our children were at home and I was traveling the world speaking, she held the fort down with excellence, stability, and strength. But she absolutely expects me to be the burden-bearer in our household; to shoulder all financial pressures; to take on the spiritual attacks; to be the protector and the provider; to make the ultimate, difficult decisions. In that sense, as much as I honor her, as much as I prefer her to myself and put her first, as much as I seek to lay my life down for her, as much as I respect her and value her and look to her, she expects me to be the head of the home. And she is not alone in feeling this way.

On several different occasions I did impromptu surveys with the students in our ministry school, all of whom feel called by God to some type of ministry service. I asked the women if they were to be married, if they would like to be the buck-stops person in the marriage, the one on whom the final responsibility would fall, the one who would be expected to take on the burden of fighting off demonic attacks and dealing with financial crises. As I conducted this survey over the years, almost none of them said yes, including the few who were already married. And remember, these are strong Christian women, mainly college-aged and single, with burning hearts to make an impact for the Lord.

In contrast, when I asked the male students the same questions (most of them are single and college-aged as well), almost all of them said yes. They felt called to take such responsibility. They even welcomed it and desired it, as do I. (I have since done this same survey at ministry gatherings with leadership couples, always with the same results.)

After all, men on average are physically bigger and stronger than women, which is one of the reasons that from the earliest human history the men were expected to care for the women, who in turn cared for the children. It was the husband who was out hunting while his pregnant wife took care of things in the home. And lest this seem too primitive an example for you (I can literally *feel* some readers rolling their eyes at these paragraphs), some conservative journalists rightly observed that in the aftermath of Hurricane Harvey in Houston, Texas, in 2017, the men were rescuing the women, who in turn, were rescuing the children.

The Acculturated website posted an article by Mark Tapson titled "Houston Rescuers Prove the Lie of 'Toxic Masculinity.'" He began his piece with sarcasm, mocking our "patriarchal privilege" and explaining how "we are the source of literally all the world's problems," from war to income inequality and from "rape culture" to "mansplaining" and "manspreading." How evil we males are! "If we are ever to create a nonviolent, truly gender-equal world," he writes, "we must rip away the false, culturally-constructed façade of masculinity." No more macho maleness! We must find new ways to be strong.[52]

Then, after pointing to numerous photographic examples of men acting sacrificially to save women and children, he singled out one in particular, noting that:

The image that most represents the spirit of men coming to the rescue in Texas is this one, of a Houston SWAT member carrying a young woman and her child Sunday afternoon. One woman named Renna who tweeted the photo sarcastically captioned it, "Toxic masculinity and privilege," and many commenters chimed in, praising masculinity.

"A man, behaving as a man, a real man. Thank goodness for men like him," tweeted one.

Another tweeted, "Remember this the next time self-righteous women talk about 'toxic masculinity.' Thank you brave heroes of #Houston and God bless our troops."[53]

And do you think there's a good reason that the most dangerous jobs in America, from logging to roofing to driving trucks, are worked overwhelmingly by men?[54]

Without a doubt the Bible praises strong female leaders, such as Deborah in Judges 4–5 or the godly wife in Proverbs 31. And there are New Testament couples like Priscilla and Aquila, where the wife's name is normally put first and where it is recorded that they both instructed Apollos.[55] There is even debate as to whether a woman named Junia was considered to be an apostle (not one of the first twelve, but another early, apostolic leader).[56] And there have been pioneering, fearless female leaders like Catherine Booth of the Salvation Army, who stood side by side with their husbands.[57] But the overwhelming pattern of Scripture points to male headship in the home and in the church,[58] and Jezebel will have none of it.

This is not to say that godly women who resist oppressive male authority are "Jezebels." It is not to deny that the church has often failed to release women into their calling, nor is it to deny that Christian men often take on the worst characteristics of machismo masculinity, as if selfishness equals headship and as if husbands were called to dominate their wives rather than serve them.

And without question there are many things women do better than men. On average, women are more sensitive, more compassionate, and more nurturing, just to give a few examples. That's why there are quite a few professions in which women tend to be predominant, including aspects of healthcare and children's education,[59] and that's why there will always be exceptional female leaders like former British Prime Minister Margaret Thatcher. Ronald Reagan had nothing on her.

And putting aside radical feminist rhetoric, there are "toxic masculinities" to be repented of and destructive patriarchal habits that hurt women rather than help them. But one of the greatest problems in our society today is that many men—I'm speaking in particular of Christian men—are failing to take their spiritual and moral responsibility, failing to lead with courage, failing to set godly examples in their homes, failing to speak up and stand up, failing to control their anger and their lust, failing to fulfill their calling.[60]

This makes Jezebel smile. The more that males are emasculated, the happier she is. She can already sense the kill.

To quote Andrea Dworkin again (from her novel *Mercy*), "Any man will follow any feminine looking thing down any dark alley; I've always wanted to see a man beaten to a [expletive] bloody pulp with a high-heeled shoe stuffed up his mouth, sort of the pig with the apple."[61]

This is the spirit of Jezebel: First seduce the man. Then emasculate him. Then eradicate him.

CHAPTER 7

JEZEBEL AND THE WAR ON GENDER DISTINCTIONS

BEGINNING WITH THE Stonewall riots in 1969, gay activism has transformed America like no other movement in our history, to the point that these riots—initiated when homosexual and transgender patrons of the Stonewall Inn and others resisted arrest—were actually hailed by President Barack Obama in his second inaugural speech. Delivering his message to the nation in January 2013, the president likened this violent uprising to the women's suffrage movement, unofficially launched at a July 1848 conference in Seneca Falls, New York, and the civil rights movement, which captured the nation's attention with its 1960s voting rights marches, including the one in Selma, Alabama. The alliteration was too good to pass up:

> We, the people, declare today that the most evident of truths—that all of us are created equal—is the star that guides us still; just as it guided our forebears through Seneca Falls, and Selma, and Stonewall; just as it guided all those men and women, sung and unsung, who left footprints along this great Mall, to hear a preacher say that we cannot walk alone; to hear a King proclaim that our individual freedom is inextricably bound to the freedom of every soul on Earth.[1]

Stonewall was now something to be celebrated, a landmark in American history, a source of pride for all. But just a few years earlier, when running for president in 2008, Obama stated plainly and repeatedly that marriage was the union of one man and one woman only. He was clear in his opposition to gay marriage, at least clear in terms of his public statements.

In reality, as we now know from previous statements he issued and from his campaign manager David Axelrod, Obama lied about his views so as not to alienate his black voters, who were largely conservative on issues like marriage and family.[2] By 2012 the political climate had changed sufficiently that the president could claim that his views had "evolved" and that he now supported same-sex marriage.[3] By 2015 the Supreme Court had redefined marriage to include a man "marrying" a man and a woman "marrying" a woman. Just a few years earlier this was unimaginable, even for many gay activists.

Today gay activist curricula dominate our children's schools, beginning with preschool, and drag queens read to toddlers in libraries. One of them admitted openly that they're trying to "groom" the children to think differently.[4]

Today students have been expelled from universities and workers have been fired from their jobs for daring to differ with gay activist talking points. As I began warning in 2004, those who came out of the closet have wanted to put us in the closet. They have been incredibly successful in their actions.[5]

Today in state after state it is against the law for minors with unwanted same-sex attractions to get professional counseling, with the end goal being a ban on all professional counseling for people of all ages struggling with same-sex attractions. (I dubbed the first attempt at such legislation, in California, the "Must Stay Gay" bill.)

Today you are branded a hater, a homophobe, a bigot, and a Nazi if you have any problem with a gay male couple adopting a baby girl or if you have the temerity to say the world's best dad is not a mom and the world's best mom is not a dad.

Today, as a committed Christian, you could even go to jail for refusing to issue a marriage license to a gay couple.[6]

This is just the tiny tip of a massive iceberg. A little more than ten years ago, in 2007, the *T* part of the LGBT movement was still quite marginalized, to the point that *Salon* magazine ran a story announcing that "the 30-year fight for a federal gay civil rights law may fail because activists insist on including rights for transgendered people too." This led to the question, "Has gay inclusiveness gone too far too fast?"[7]

Today elementary school children are encouraged to question their gender identity, and under President Obama high schools would lose federal funding if they refused to allow fifteen-year-old boys who identified as girls to play on the girls' sports teams and share their locker rooms.[8]

Today Twitter will ban users who identify Caitlyn Jenner as Bruce or still refer to him as "he," and teachers have lost their jobs for refusing to refer to a biological male by a female name or pronoun (or vice versa). In New York City you could be fined $250,000 for doing the same on your job.[9]

Today "Colorado residents who do not identify as male or female [are] allowed to choose X as the symbol to represent their gender on their driver's licenses,"[10] while in some states and parts of Canada those who undergo sex-change surgery can have their *birth certificates* changed.[11] But surgery isn't even necessary in some places. In fact, in New York City you can now get your birth certificate changed to X (so, neither male nor female) simply by having a notarized affidavit. That's it![12]

Today transgender rights trump women's rights, as many a feminist has now complained,[13] and academics argue that *biological sex* cannot be determined biologically.[14]

Today we hear about pregnant men, accompanied by pictures of a bearded "man" (a biological woman, now on male hormones) nursing her daughter,[15] while eight-year-olds in the UK are told that "boys can have periods too."[16]

That's because at the root of LGBT activism is a war against gender distinctions. The male-female dichotomy must be destroyed. The constricting binary must be undone. As Dr. Barb Burdge, a professor of social work at Manchester University, herself a lesbian, argues, "Binary gender models are the foundation on which transgender oppression (and several other oppressive systems) depends."[17] Or, with less hostility but the same end result, feminist Ruth Barrett writes, "There are over seven billion human beings on the planet. Therefore, there have to be over seven billion genders. No one is special if we are all unique. When you think outside the gender identity frame, the concept of gender disappears because it is irrelevant to our uniqueness."[18]

That's why a group known as "The Feminists," active from 1968 to 1973, was more fully known as "Feminists—A Political Organization to Annihilate Sex Roles."[19] And this dates back to the late 1960s! Gender distinctions themselves must be opposed, the Feminists cried. And, quite naturally, marriage must be eliminated.

As noted on Wikipedia:

> The Feminists' best-known action may have been in September 1969, when members picketed the New York City Marriage License Bureau, distributing pamphlets protesting the marriage contract: "All the discriminatory practices against women are patterned and rationalized by this slavery-like practice. We can't destroy the inequities between men and women until we destroy marriage."[20]

In a very real way, then, this too is a manifestation of the spirit of Jezebel, since she emasculates men, turning them into emotionally castrated males, and she defeminizes women, turning them into male-hating lesbians.[21] This way, she destroys the God-ordained roles for males and females, thereby destroying the very foundations of our society. Can you see how all of this fits together?

RADICAL FEMINISM AND NEUTERED MEN

In the last chapter I explained how radical feminism neuters men (quoting Allen West), also mentioning that men who impregnate women but do not take responsibility for the children are not acting like real men. As a result these children are born without a male role model, which can lead to all kinds of potentially negative effects. Studies indicate that girls raised without a father tend to be more promiscuous, while boys raised without a father tend to have higher rates of delinquency.[22] Not only so, but as I have heard many counselors testify and many ex-gays affirm, the absence of a father (or the presence of a weak father) can heighten the potential of male homosexual development for a number of reasons.[23]

As explained in 2004 by Dr. Joseph Nicolosi, perhaps the best known proponent of this theory:

> Recent political pressure has resulted in a denial of the importance of the factor most strongly implicated by decades of previous clinical research—*developmental factors, particularly the influence of parents.* A review of the literature on male homosexuality reveals extensive reference to the prehomosexual boy's relational problems with both parents (West 1959, Socarides 1978, Evans 1969); among some researchers, the father-son

relationship has been particularly implicated (Bieber et al 1962, Moberly 1983)....

Nonmasculine or feminine behavior in boyhood has been repeatedly shown to be correlated with later homosexuality (Green, 1987, Zuger, 1988); taken together with related factors—particularly the often-reported alienation from same-sex peers and *poor relationship with father*—this suggests a failure to fully gender-identify. In its more extreme form, this same syndrome (usually resulting in homosexuality) is diagnosed as Childhood Gender-Identity Deficit (Zucker and Bradley, 1996).[24]

This does not mean that parents (or the absence of certain parents) "make" their children gay or that there's an easy, cookie-cutter explanation for all homosexual development. And it certainly doesn't imply that a child "chose" to be gay as some kind of overt psychological reaction. Far from it.

But it does suggest that weak or absentee fathers can contribute negatively to their child's sexual and emotional development (is this any surprise?), which in turn can result in sexual and romantic confusion. That's why it doesn't surprise me that there's a growing crisis of male homosexuality in the African American community (when hidden, it's called "down low," or DL for short) at the same that there is a crisis of fatherlessness in that same community.

On the issue of fatherlessness, Walter E. Williams, a professor of economics at George Mason University and himself an African American, pointed to the tremendous deterioration of the black American family in recent generations. Writing in 2015, he noted that by the 1880s, barely two decades after the Civil War, "three-quarters of black families were two-parent."

By 1925, in New York City, "85 percent of black families were two-parent." He even cited a study of nineteenth-century slave families. Strikingly, in as many as 75 percent of these families, "all the children had the same mother and father."[25]

In stark contrast Williams pointed out that in 2015 "the overwhelming majority" of African American children were being raised by single mothers, and the percentage of black out-of-wedlock births stood at 75 percent, something that was "entirely new." What a shift! As of 1940, according to Williams, only 14 percent of black children were born to unmarried parents. He explained that "both during slavery and as late as 1920, a teenage girl raising a child without a man present was rare among blacks."[26] Even as of 1965 the percentage had risen only to 25. That's the year Senator Daniel Patrick Moynihan wrote *The Negro Family: The Case for National Action*, and he "was widely condemned as a racist."[27] By 1980 out-of-wedlock births had more than doubled among African Americans to 56 percent, and the percentage keeps increasing. Isn't this devastating?

On the issue of being "down low" in black America, one African American pastor referred to it as an "invisible disease,"[28] and these shocking statistics from the Centers for Disease Control would seem to confirm this: "Black/African American gay and bisexual men are more affected by HIV than any other group in the United States. In 2017, black/African American gay and bisexual men accounted for 26% (10,070) of the 38,739 new HIV diagnoses and 37% of new diagnoses among all gay and bisexual men in the United States and dependent areas."[29]

Yet it gets worse: "Young, black MSM (aged 13–24 years) [the abbreviation *MSM* means "men who have sex with men"]—the most severely affected subpopulation of MSM—accounted for more new diagnoses in the United States (3,888 in 2015) than any other subgroup by race/ethnicity, age and sex."[30]

Citing these statistics, I get a sick feeling in the pit of my stomach as I see how the enemy wants to destroy black Americans, who for the record tend to have a higher percentage of church attendance and Christian profession than the rest of the population.[31] And to be candid, it's hard for me *not* to connect the dots between a dangerous spike in fatherlessness in the African American community and a spike in (largely hidden) homosexual practice, especially among young men.

Again, I blame the devil for this more than anyone. (Some would also argue that the welfare system contributes directly to the phenomenon of fatherlessness; I'll let others debate that controversial issue.[32]) And I see this as yet another part of Satan's multipronged strategy to destroy this precious and important part of our population. (If you're an African American reader, please hear me loudly and clearly: I'm standing *with* you against our common enemy, Satan, believing that there is a great, nation-changing calling on your community, which is why the enemy so hates you.)

We also see the devil's strategy in the disproportionate percentage of black American abortions, which is why websites such as blackgenocide.org exist. It states, "The purpose of this web site is to expose the disproportionate amount of Black babies destroyed by the abortion industry."[33] According to the 2019 National Right to Life "State of Abortion" report, among black women there are 390 abortions for every 1,000 live births, meaning a little less than 4 out of 10 pregnancies are aborted.[34]

Again, these are devastating statistics—really, what's devastating is that these statistics are about *human beings*—but the picture continues to come into focus. There *is* a connection between sexual immorality, baby killing, fatherlessness, homosexuality, and the breakdown of gender distinctions and roles. As two conservative researchers noted:

> *The pathologies and moral crises of our era do not stand in isolation. They are entwined, inextricably.* The pound of flesh demanded by Shylock from Antonio in "The Merchant of Venice" could not be removed without the loss of Antonio's blood. The veins of the victim, laced throughout his body, were impossible to segregate from the flesh itself. So it is with the intersecting layers of family life, human sexual behavior, public policy, and the well-being of our children.[35]

STEP BACK AND THINK ABOUT IT

To repeat: there's a reason that over the course of one generation we have seen exponential increases in sexual immorality, abortion, radical feminism, homosexuality, and the abolition of gender distinctions. It is hardly a coincidence. Instead, it is the consequence of our lack of connection with the Lord, the fruit of idolatry, the result of a Jezebelian attack. When you step back for a moment and look, the picture becomes quite clear. Even Mormon leader Dallin H. Oaks observed that it is Satan who "seeks to confuse gender, to distort marriage, and to discourage childbearing—especially by parents who will raise children in truth."[36]

Already in 1968, one year before the Stonewall riots and early in the rise of radical feminism, Francis Schaeffer had already pinpointed the problem in his book *The God Who Is There.* "But much modern homosexuality," he wrote, "is an expression of the current denial of antithesis. It has led in this case to an obliteration of the distinction between man and woman. So the male and the female as complementary partners are finished."[37] Schaeffer observed this *more than fifty years ago.* Can we not see it today?

I have documented the nature of transgender activism and the ongoing war on gender for almost fifteen years, feeling nothing but love for those who struggle and wanting only God's best for them. But love also motivates us to stand up for what is right, to protect our children from aggressive and unhelpful indoctrination, to protest unfair and even dangerous policies, and to speak the truth, even when it's unpopular.

In 2014 I wrote an article titled "Why LGBT's War on Gender Must Be Resisted,"[38] noting that there was an outright war on gender today and explaining that for some years now it had been an essential part of LGBT activism. If it succeeded, I wrote, it would make gender distinctions all but meaningless.

You see, the moment gay activists attempted to redefine marriage, they also rendered gender meaningless within marriage, since for them marriage was no longer the union of a man and a woman but the union of any two people, irrespective of gender. And once you render gender meaningless within marriage, you render it meaningless in society as a whole.

That's why gay activist organizations like GLSEN (the Gay, Lesbian & Straight Education Network) have actively worked against gender distinctions in our children's schools, as if gender itself has become the enemy. That's why, to cite one example of many, in Lafayette, California, kids in a sex-ed class "used a diagram called the 'Genderbread Person' to teach students that they could be 'agender,' 'bigender,' 'third gender,' 'two spirit,' and 'gender queer.'"[39]

Gay activists support this passionately, to the point that we are now told that *T* (meaning transgender) is the new black, the new face of the civil rights movement. And if you dare speak up against the growing war on gender, you are branded a transphobic bigot.

How far will this war on gender go? A December 5, 2014, article told the story of Mary Ann Barclay, a professing lesbian who has now undergone "gender transition" to become "a non-binary person," meaning neither male nor female.[40] This is becoming increasingly common.

To be sure, we should have compassion on people in their struggles, also recognizing that there are some real exceptions to the simple male-female categories, such as people with biological or chromosomal abnormalities. But the existence of the exception doesn't negate the rule. Instead, the exception proves the rule.

Also in 2014 Dr. Al Mohler stated in a radio commentary that "the elimination of gender distinctions, in terms of biological gender identity assigned at birth, is something that will lead to a massive confusion at the very heart of what it means to be human."[41] How could it be otherwise?

Back in 2014 Facebook yielded to transgender activists who protested the all-too-confining "male" and "female" choices on the personal bio page, adding fifty ways to describe your gender, including ten simultaneously. (That's right, you could simultaneously choose to identify as male, female, genderqueer, and seven other options.) Really now, if I offered you one million dollars to come up with fifty gender descriptions, could you? How about twenty-five? Maybe ten? Most of us would be hard pressed to do so. But it turns out fifty was not enough. Facebook had to add one more option: "Fill in the blank."[42] I kid you not.

In 2011 one of my colleagues compiled this list of gender descriptions and sexual orientations: androgeny, androgenous, bigendered, bi-dyke, boi, boidyke (or, boydyke), bro-sis, butch, butchdyke, camp, cross-dresser (CD), cross-living, drag (in drag), drag king, drag queen, dyke, FTM or F->M or F2M (Female to Male), femme, femme dyke, female bodied, female impersonator (FI), fetishistic transvestite, gender illusionist, gender neutral, gender-bender, gender-blender, genderqueer, genetic boy, genetic male/man (GM), genetic female/woman (GF/GW), genetic girl (GG), grrl, half-dyke, heteroflexible, hir, intersex, MTF or M->F or M2F (Male to Female), male impersonator, metamorph, monogendered, multigendered, neuter, no-gendered, non-op, omnisexual, pansexual, pre-operative transsexual (pre-op TS), polygendered, post-operative transsexual, queer, queerboi, shape shifter, stem (a feminine-identified lesbian), stud (a masculine-identified lesbian), trannyboi, trannydyke, trannyfag, transboi, transgendered, transgenderist, transitioning, transmale, transsexual (TS), transvestite, transidentified, trisexual, two-spirit, ze.[43] I'm sure it has grown since 2011.

One young man has stated, "I'm a Gender Smoothie. Just take everything about gender, throw it in the blender, press the button, and that's me."[44] Another student has preferred not to be identified as male or female but instead prefers to be called Tractor.[45]

Today, on an increasing number of college campuses, professors are required to ask students how they want to be identified. Pronoun options include:

- ve/vis/vir/verself

- jee/jem/jeir/jemself

- lee/lim/lis/limself

- kye/kyr/kyne/kyrself

- per/per/pers/perself
- hu/hum/hus/humself
- bun/bun/buns/bunself
- it/it/its/itself

With all due compassion for those who genuinely struggle with their gender identity, this is collaborating with madness, and it naturally leads to a situation where some people identify as part animal or part alien. After all, if perception is reality and if something as fundamental as male-female distinctions becomes malleable, why not?[46]

It's no surprise that in recent years we have not only seen the rise of same-sex marriage but of other distortions and perversions of God-ordained marriage, including polyamory, multiple loving partners in any number or configuration); polygamy, which is gaining popularity in America, no doubt with the help of shows such as *Big Love, Sister Wives,* and *My Five Wives*; sologamy, marrying oneself (there is a growing network to serve those doing so); throuples, three men, three women, or three people with a mixture of genders; marrying robots; marrying animals (from snakes to dogs to dolphins); and marrying inanimate objects (from the Eiffel Tower—just search for Erika Eiffel—to a computer, or at least a man tried without success to marry his computer).[47] There's a reason for this wise warning of Walter Dean Burnham: "A wise man does not tear down a fence until he learns why it was put up."[48]

On December 13, 2018, Bill Muehlenberg, an American who has been living in Australia for many years and is a prophetic voice to the culture, posted an article titled "The Terrorism of Trans Tyranny."[49] In the article, he listed five recent examples of this tyranny. They were:

1. A teacher in Virginia lost his job because he refused to refer to a female student by male pronouns.[50]

2. "A UK professor has received a barrage of abuse after suggesting a woman is defined by law as biological, not psychological."[51]

3. A "Canadian man claiming to be 'female' sues 16 women for refusing to wax his genitals."[52]

4. "A six-year-old Texas boy is being dressed and presented as a girl by his mother; at the same time, she is threatening the boy's father legally for not going along with her plan for their son to live as a girl. James lives as a girl when with his mother, but when with his father and given the choice, the six-year-old boy lives as a boy."[53]

5. "A Minnesota mother is appealing a judge's decision to dismiss her lawsuit against school authorities who gave her teenage son female hormone treatments without her permission."[54]

For good reason, Muehlenberg notes, "I have already written books about how much people have suffered and been abused by the homosexual agenda in full swing. Now it looks like I need to write more books on how the new trans tyranny is destroying everything it touches. If I do, by the time it gets into print it will already be out of date." He concluded, "Such is the rate of downward decline in the West."[55] He is not overstating things in the least.

The bottom line is that the same Jezebelian spirit that wants to distort the meaning of male and female also wants to destroy the meaning of male and female. That's why Dennis

Prager was right to protest the trend against gender-specific toys in 2015.[56] He pointed that more important than academic research on sex differences was the research conducted by businesses and advertising agencies. Why? It's because "their agenda is profit," and if their assessments are not on target, they lose money and those doing the poor research are fired. Academics, on the other hand, lose nothing if they publish nonsense that their colleagues affirm.

Interestingly, research done by Mattel indicated that "male nature wants good guys to kill bad guys (of course, in bad societies the definition of 'good guy' and 'villain' may well be inverted, but that is a values issue, not a male-nature issue); and that female nature wants the good guy and bad guy to 'be friends in the end.'"[57] Why was this so important? After giving lots of examples, Prager explained that because each sex has its own distinct nature, each sex needs the other: "Men need women to soften their intrinsic aggressive nature and to help them control their predatory sexuality; and women need men to, among other things, better understand that evil people and regimes must be fought, not nurtured." That's why he urged his readers to pay attention to Mattel's research, noting that out of all the destructive things that the Left has done to America, "it is quite possible that none will prove to be more destructive than its attempt to obliterate gender distinctions."[58]

It's time to connect the dots. In fact, it's well past time. The picture is already emerging with clarity and force. We deny it to our own peril and to the peril of our children.

And if somehow, some way, you think I'm exaggerating, as if I was engaging in Chicken Little histrionics and claiming the sky is falling, I'll allow a journalist on the Left, George Gillett, to speak for himself. As the headline proclaims, "We Shouldn't Fight for 'Gender Equality'. We Should Fight to Abolish

Gender." Yes, "Gender is flawed—no set of social scripts will ever represent the wonderful diversity and intricacy of human behaviour."[59]

He argues that "the existence of gender itself is, by definition, inherently oppressive," by which he means the existence of societal distinctions and expectations based on biological sex. Therefore, he concludes that:

> [With each gender stereotype that is eliminated] we move a step closer towards equality and liberation. But instead of trudging along the laborious and indirect path of eliminating these stereotypes one at a time, we should be clear and proud of our aims. Indeed, the façade of "redefining" masculinity and femininity isn't a compromise, it's a contradiction. The aim of "gender equality" doesn't go far enough—we need to confront the very concept of gender itself.[60]

Does it need to be spelled out any more plainly?

But let me remind you again: there is a price to pay for challenging Jezebel. There is an attack that will come your way. That's why, often on a daily basis, I receive death wishes and the ugliest, most perverse attacks imaginable, simply for saying that Jesus can set people free from homosexual practice or that God in His love wants to help transgenders from the inside out.

For making comments like these, I have been told I should burn to death, die a slow and painful death, die of various forms of cancer, be assassinated, or be beaten over the head with a Bible until I have nerve damage—and that is just to list a few. To quote one of these lovely comments directly, in response to our animated video "Can You Be Gay and Christian?,"[61] someone posted: "Burn this guy at the stake or do whatever yall want i dont give a [expletive]. Just make sure he suffers before he dies. okay? Okay."[62]

But what else should we expect? The darkness hates the light, and Jesus told us that the world would treat us the same way it treated Him. (See Matthew 10:24–25; John 15:18–20.)

So what will we do? I say we speak the truth in love. I say we stand up and push back with grace, courage, and respect. I say, in the name of Jesus and in the power of the Spirit, hidden in the Word and clothed with God's armor, we face down Jezebel in our day.

What do you say?

CHAPTER 8

JEZEBEL AND THE RISE OF WITCHCRAFT

On December 16, 2018, I did a Google search for the phrase "the rise of witchcraft in America." These were some of the top stories that came up:

- "The US Witch Population Has Seen an Astronomical Rise" (posted October 4, 2018)[1]

- "Surveys Find Witchcraft Is on the Rise Across America" (posted October 10, 2018)[2]

- "Report: Witchcraft Rising in US as Christianity Declines" (posted October 11, 2018)[3]

- "Number of Witches Rises Dramatically Across U.S. as Millennials Reject Christianity" (posted November 18, 2018)[4]

- "Witches Outnumbers Presbyterians Among U.S. Millennials" (posted October 11, 2018)[5]

- "Number of Americans Who Say They Are Witches Is on the Rise" (posted October 30, 2018)[6]

- "Why Millennials Are Ditching Religion for Witchcraft and Astrology" (posted October 31, 2018)[7]

- "There Are Now More Practicing Witches in the U.S. Than Ever Before" (posted November 19, 2018)[8]

- "The Fastest Growing Religion in America Is Witchcraft" (posted October 30, 2013, indicating that this has been going on for some time)[9]

Do I have your attention now? Can you deny that the spirit of Jezebel, the woman known for her sorceries and witchcraft (see again 2 Kings 9:22), is thriving in America today? Can you deny the connection between: 1) our turning away from the one true God after idols; 2) the massive spike in pornography and immorality; 3) the militant, child-killing spirit; 4) radical feminism; 5) the aggressive LGBT movement; and 6) the sudden rise in witchcraft?

This has Jezebel's name written all over it in all caps, boldly and clearly. And does it mean nothing that in early 2018 it was announced that *500 million* Harry Potter books—books glorifying sorcery and wizardry—have now been sold worldwide, even if much of the content is relatively "innocent"?[10] Just watch the children participating at the massive Wizarding World of Harry Potter area in a theme park in Orlando. They too want to be wizards and sorcerers.

As if more confirmation was needed, just as I had written these very words—meaning the words of the previous two paragraphs—I looked at my Twitter account and spotted a new tweet from my colleague Dr. James White saying, "It is very hard not to see a strong spirit of deception and delusion working in this culture—we murder our babies, destroy the gift of marriage, even mutilate young children all in service to the god of human autonomy. But, the judgment is just."[11]

In 2007 Yoko Ono, the widow of John Lennon, made this comment while talking about her new CD project, titled *Yes, I'm a Witch*:

> I think that all women are witches, in the sense that a witch is a magical being. And a wizard, which is a male version of a witch, is kind of revered, and people respect wizards. But a witch, my god, we have to burn

them. It's the male chauvinistic society that we're living in for the longest time, 3,000 years or whatever. And so I just wanted to point out the fact that men and women are magical beings. We are very blessed that way, so I'm just bringing that out. Don't be scared of witches, because we are good witches, and you should appreciate our magical power.[12]

Even if we acknowledge some hyperbole in Ono's words, and even if we recognize that she's not talking about satanist witches who literally sacrifice children on bloody altars, there's no denying the clear import of her words: witchcraft and radical feminism are closely connected, joined together in their rejection of "the male chauvinistic society."

At the beginning of her book *Radical Feminism: Feminist Activism in Movement*, Finn Mackay offers this fascinating account from West Germany:

In the midst of the Cold War, in a divided country, feminists were about to start a global movement that for decades to come would unite women in symbolic protest against male violence against women. Shortly before midnight on 30 April 1977, small groups of women began gathering in the centre of towns and cities across West Germany: Bochum, Frankfurt, Cologne, Hanau. They were dressed as witches, carried flaming torches and had painted women's symbols on their faces. The date of their synchronised protest was no accident. They were assembling on that night to mark what is still known across Germany as Walpurgis Night, a superstitious tradition to mark the coming of May; a time when witches and tricksters are believed to roam.[13]

So a global feminist movement was birthed on the night "when witches and tricksters are believed to roam," and the women even dressed as witches. To call this a coincidence is to strain credulity.

Again, this does not mean all the women involved were given over to witchcraft in its ugliest, darkest aspects, nor does it mean much of their cause was not justified, namely, protesting male violence against women. In that respect I stand with them, as I stand with them in fighting for many of the causes discussed in Mackay's book. But I stand *against* the spirit of radical feminism and *against* the spirit of witchcraft, which are in many ways two sides of the same coin.

Is it any wonder that as of February 5, 2019, the most prominent graphic featured on Mackay's website was a chart listing twenty ways for "Raising Children Without Gender Stereotypes"[14] or that one her most recent talks listed was titled "Beyond Men and Women"? The description read, "Traditional categories of male and female are being eroded. But if we could see a world beyond gender, would we want it?"[15]

The dots are all connected. The picture is there to see. Ahab's queen lives on.

SEASON OF THE WITCH

I noted in chapter 6 that Rebecca Traister's book on the power of female rage, *Good and Mad*, was hardly a mindless screed. Yet the third part of the book is titled "Season of the Witch."[16] This is ironic, to say the least.

Now, if you're like me, you want to see solid evidence before you make a judgment. You want to be convinced. And you might be saying to yourself, "It seems hard to deny the connection between radical feminism and witchcraft, but are we stretching things a little to fit a preconceived theory?" Honestly, I believe the evidence is overwhelming and compelling. The dots really do connect.

But if you still have some doubts, maybe this HuffPost article will persuade you, dated December 23, 2018, and titled "2018 Was the Year American Women Embraced Their Inner Witch." That is quite the headline! The article by Lily Burana refers to the "Season of the Witch," explaining while some witches are male, "the latest upsurge in witchcraft is largely a chick-and-genderfluid thing—a spiritual seeking turbocharged by affinity with the supernatural and belief in the sacred feminine and the divine androgyne."[17]

And then come these words, almost as if Burana had been reading over my shoulder as I wrote the pages of this book, citing an article in *Boston Review* written by Jesse Kindig and describing the 1968 manifesto of the women's liberation activist group W.I.T.C.H. (standing for "Women's International Terrorist Conspiracy from Hell"). Kindig noted that the manifesto proposed that "'a witch lives and laughs in every woman. She is the free part of each of us.' It is this history—from 1486 on—that explains today's global feminist protest chant, 'We are the granddaughters of all the witches you could not burn!'"[18] Oh my!

There is nothing hidden or subtle here in the least, just an integral connection between radical feminism and witchcraft. Burana also connects witchcraft to "female power, resistance," to the woman "bowed by no man," to "an untamed spirit," noting that while there have always been witches, "now she's re-emerging as a cultural and political force with an aesthetic and an agenda."[19]

Need I say more? The dots have connected themselves clearly. In fact, in some cases we don't need to connect the dots. The letters have spelled things out for us, explicitly and without ambiguity, as in the radical feminist group just mentioned, W.I.T.C.H.[20] Or shall I mention the radical feminist (and lesbian) group that calls itself the [Expletive] Church of Modern Witchcraft?[21]

In the last chapter I stated that Jezebel emasculates men, turning them into emotionally castrated males, and she defeminizes women, turning them into male-hating lesbians. Is it any wonder, then, that on November 24, 2017, Finn Mackay tweeted, "Exciting! Had my paper on #butch #lesbian identity accepted for the BSA Conference next year #Sociology #gender #gnc #masculinities #feminism #moc"?[22] Or should we be surprised that on August 20, 2018, she posted an article titled "Whose [sic] Afraid of Female Masculinity?"[23]

More than twenty years ago, while participating in an Operation Rescue event at an abortion clinic near Washington, DC, I was struck by the composition of those protesting our presence. The most prominent among them were atheists, satanists, and gays and lesbians. What a coalition![24]

It also brought a question to mind: Why were gays and lesbians so upset about a pro-life protest? Why were they so adamantly proabortion? (Adamant enough, it turns out, to get advance notice of where we would be and showing up there very early in the morning.) Since gay and lesbian sex is not procreative, you would think abortion would not be a major concern for them. But there they were, joined with atheists and satanists, cursing us for our stand for life.

Friends of mine active on a weekly basis at abortion clinics have told me this threefold coalition of death is as strong as ever. The one added ingredient is this: witches have also taken a more prominent proabortion, anti-life role.

As *Newsweek* reported on October 22, 2018, about two weeks after Brett Kavanaugh was confirmed to the Supreme Court, opponents of Kavanaugh gathered "to observe and perform a hex in the hope that it would cause him to suffer."[25] The article went on to say:

> If Dakota Bracciale, co-owner of Catland Books, where the hex was hosted, could write the headline for the event, it would read as follows, "Witches gather to weather the storm, take no [expletive] and do all the harm."
>
> "If [the hex] causes suffering and harm and trouble and chaos and mayhem for anyone in the GOP, I'm happy," Bracciale told *Newsweek*.[26]

Witches trying to curse a presumably pro-life justice? Is this another coincidence? Hardly. In an article dated November 10, 2018, Linda Harvey spoke of "Witches at the Abortion Clinic 'Blessing.'" She asked, "How deeply are abortion clinics connected to witchcraft?" Her answer: "Christians from all over Ohio who stood together to protest a 'sacred blessing' ceremony at a Columbus, Ohio abortion clinic on November 9 discovered the volunteers and staff may be quite involved.... They discovered evidence of sorcery and symbols of witchcraft rituals performed before they arrived."[27] And in anticipation of chapter 10 I should also point out that "each month, thousands of witches cast a spell against Donald Trump."[28]

Looking at the recent spike in interest in sorcery, wizardry, and witchcraft, it's only fair to ask how much of it is serious. How much of it is truly dark and satanic? How much of it is children playing make-believe with wands, and how much of it is a portal into deception and demonization? At the very least this stuff is a portal into false spirituality, a portal away from biblical truth. Or do you think the Bible is used as a textbook in the real-life school of wizardry now open in Poland?[29] A lot of the stuff at the College of Wizardry is just fantasy role-playing, but it is certainly a step in the wrong direction.

And what are we to make of headlines like these, the result of a search for "the rise in the occult in America"?

- "What's Behind the Seemingly Unrelenting Rise of Satanism?" (posted January 19, 2017)[30]

- "Rise of Satanism Another Sign of 'America's Fall From God'" (posted September 27, 2016)[31]

- "American Society 'Submerged' in the Occult, Says Ex-Satanist" (posted March 8, 2013)[32]

- "What the [Expletive]? Satan Worship on Rise in America" (posted August 29, 2016)[33]

- "The Rise of Satanism in America" (posted January 21, 2019)[34]

Writing in 2000, Richard Kyle noted:

In 1967 [the Broadway musical] *Hair* exploded like a bomb on the American cultural scene. This hit musical production revealed to the "straight" world that a new world was coming. The Age of Pisces—the era of Christianity, rationalism, and science—would soon be replaced by the Age of Aquarius. This new golden age was to be one of peace, brotherhood, progress, mysticism, and occult knowledge.[35]

And note where Kyle locates some of the pivotal years for this change: 1969–1970, the exact same time radical feminism and gay liberation were finding their stride. He writes:

> But in the late sixties and seventies, the occult became a passion for some and a fad for many. *Time*'s cover story of March 21, 1969, "Cult of the Occult," gave an indication of the large number of people involved in the occult phenomenon. During 1969 and 1970, *Harper's Bazaar, Esquire,* and *McCall's* had special issues on the occult revival. Many institutions of higher learning, including prestigious universities, began to offer courses on aspects of the occult. Universities and institutes sponsored research on parapsychological phenomena.[36]

Speaking in 2013, ex-satanist Jeff Harshbarger, head of Refuge Ministries and author of the book *Dancing With the Devil,* said this: "Our society is submerged in the occult; Harry Potter has filled the minds of our children for a decade and vampirism meets our teens with the illusions of grandeur. Witchcraft went mainstream decades ago, and Wicca is its offspring." Yes, even "'Christian' witchcraft is on the up-rise and new age spirituality fills the church pews."[37]

Perhaps it's no coincidence that we're also seeing headlines such as "US Exorcists: Demonic Activity on the Rise." According to the article, "there is an alarming increase in demonic activity being reported by those who work in exorcism ministry, said the exorcist for the Archdiocese of Indianapolis. Although steps are being taken to increase the number of exorcists, demand is still outpacing supply."[38]

Sociologist Rodney Stark pointed out that in European countries where church attendance is especially low, Christian faith has not been replaced by secularism. It has been replaced by superstition! A case in point would be Iceland, considered by many sociologists of religion to be one of the most secularized nations in the world, a nation with minimal church attendance. According to a 2015 poll, "0.0% of Icelanders 25 years or younger believe God created the world," an absolutely shocking statistic.[39]

What, then, do Icelanders believe? According to Stark:

> 34 percent of Icelanders believe in reincarnation and another 16 percent aren't sure about it. Moreover, a national survey found that 55 percent of Icelanders believe in the existence of *huldufolk*, or hidden people, such as elves, trolls, gnomes, and fairies. Consequently, planned highways are sometimes rerouted so as not to disturb various hills and large rocks wherein *huldufolk* may dwell, and Icelanders planning to build a new house often hire "elf spotters" to ensure that their site does not encroach on *huldufolk* settlements. In addition, half of Icelanders have visited a fortune teller, and spiritualism is very widely practiced; it is popular even among intellectuals and academics. According to a Reuters dispatch (February 2, 2015), a rapidly growing group of Icelandic neo-pagans broke ground for a temple dedicated to worship of the old Norse gods.[40]

This confirms the words commonly misattributed to Chesterton, namely, "When people stop believing in God, they don't believe in nothing—they believe in anything."[41]

EXCHANGING LIGHT FOR DARKNESS

Paul boasted of how the Thessalonians had turned *away* from idols *to* the one true God (1 Thess. 1:9). Today America (along with Europe) has been turning *away* from the one true God, which means turning *to* false gods and idols. (This is not rocket science. If I am facing north with my back to the south, when I turn toward the south, I turn away from the north.)

Accordingly, as Paul outlined in Romans 1, as we have rejected the truth of God, we have been given over to intellectual foolishness, to sexual immorality, to homosexuality, and to a culture of death (vv. 18–32). Accordingly, one headline, cited previously, proclaimed, "Number of Witches Rises Dramatically Across U.S. *as Millennials Reject Christianity*" (emphasis added). Another article claimed to explain "Why Millennials Are Ditching Religion for Witchcraft and Astrology." This is perfectly logical. We have exchanged darkness for light and truth for error. We have chosen witchcraft and the occult and satanism rather than holiness and intimacy with God. We have followed Jezebel into idolatry. And with it we have imbibed the spirit of pornography, the spirit of baby-killing, the spirit that declares war on gender, the spirit that wants to abolish marriage, the spirit of destruction.

Again, I understand that some of the fascination of wizardry and witchcraft is relatively innocent, meaning it is hardly given over to conjuring up demons and inviting satanic possession. But none of it is good, and some of it is downright evil and dangerous.

Consider this October 29, 2016, article from Alex Mar titled "Witches of America: How I Became Immersed in a Growing Movement" and published in the UK *Guardian*. Mar begins by setting the stage for a meeting he personally attended.

Some four hundred people, all barefoot, were crammed into a darkened hotel ballroom, "listening to the sound of heavy drumming."[42]

> The hotel was flooded with about 2,000 American witches…and nearly a quarter of them—from teenagers to septuagenarians—were immersed in a ceremony led by Morpheus Ravenna, a rising pagan priestess. They had been called, with ceremonial daggers and invocations, to form a consecrated circle. Under dimmed lights, there had been full-voiced chanting as the witches "raised power" to welcome their deity into the carpeted space.[43]

What was their focus that night? "The ritual was a devotional to the Morrigan, the heavyweight Celtic goddess of war, prophecy and self-transformation. In the center of the circle, surrounded by her ritual crew, stood Morpheus, with all eyes on her." Morpheus was the name of the lead witch, who quickly began to manifest signs of demonic possession: "Her slender body doubled over, as if suddenly heavy, and began bobbing up and down as if something was bubbling up inside her."[44]

Morpheus then cried out that she was an ancient Celtic goddess, and then the witches moved in closer around her. After this "a fellow priestess lifted a heavy sword above our heads: she directed us to take a vow. 'But only if it's one you can keep. Don't take it lightly.' As Morpheus (or the goddess she was channeling) continued heaving, breathing hard, hundreds of people crowded in, taking turns to raise their hand up and touch the tip of the blade."[45]

This is hardly childlike and innocent. This is not simply playing with wands. This is playing with fire.

Mar, who also wrote a book called *Witches of America*, hailed by the *New York Times* in 2015 as notable,[46] said this:

> Since the 1960s, the "pagan" movement—what most people are referring to when they talk about American witchcraft today—has grown into a hard-to-dismiss new religious movement. In this country alone, a responsible estimate places the number of self-identified witches (typically called pagan priests and priest-esses) at about one million—comparable to those of Seventh-Day Adventists and Jehovah's Witnesses.[47]

This movement is even invading the church, with professing "Christian witches" on the increase.[48] I kid you not. Yes, these are professing Christians who claim to engage in nonsatanic witchcraft!

The spirit of Jezebel is on the rise and poised to dominate the culture, and there is only one thing Jezebel fears: the prophetic voice of the church. That's why she is dead set on silencing us, seducing us, intimidating us, emasculating us, eradicating us. In the name and authority of Jesus, I declare that she will not succeed. The wicked witch *will* be defeated, and many of those she has led into deception and captivity *will* be delivered.

CHAPTER 9

JEZEBEL AND THE SILENCING OF THE PROPHETS

THERE IS A striking account found in 1 Kings 22. By that time, several years had passed since Elijah called down fire from heaven on Mount Carmel, several years since he killed the four hundred fifty false prophets, several years since he ran from the threats of Jezebel.

Ahab, the husband of Jezebel, was still king, and once again he was surrounded by false prophets, four hundred in number. Each one of them was deceived. Each one of them gave false assurances of peace. Each one of them was misleading the king.

On this occasion Ahab was accompanied by Jehoshaphat, the godly but sometimes unwise king of Judah. They were about to join together in battle against a common foe when Jehoshaphat suggested they first inquire of Yahweh through the prophets.

Ahab asked them, "Shall I go against Ramoth Gilead to battle, or shall I wait?" (1 Kings 22:6). With one voice they all replied, "Go up, for the Lord shall deliver it into the hand of the king" (v. 6). But this got Jehoshaphat's attention. It was not just their unanimously positive word. It was the fact that they did not use Yahweh's name, speaking only of "the Lord" (*Adonai* in Hebrew).

So Jehoshaphat asked Ahab, "Is there not a prophet of the LORD [meaning Yahweh] here whom we can ask?" (v. 7).[1] Ahab replied, "There is still one man, Micaiah the son of Imlah, by whom we can inquire of the LORD [again, meaning Yahweh]. But I hate him because he never prophesies good for me, but always evil" (v. 8).

That says it all. Ahab hated this true prophet because, as the NLT reads, "He never prophesies anything but trouble for me!" But what else could Ahab expect? He did bad things, and therefore bad things would happen to him. He practiced wickedness, and he would therefore reap the fruit of wickedness. Micaiah was telling the truth—the inevitable, undeniable truth.

It was the false prophets who told the wicked that all would be well, who strengthened the hands of evildoers, who discouraged the righteous, who threw a wet blanket on the fires of repentance, who themselves indulged the flesh while comforting others who did the same. Of course they had good words for wicked Ahab, and of course Micaiah, the sole true voice, prophesied judgment.

The entire story is fascinating, but we can't recount it here in full, so you might want to take a few minutes to read the rest of that chapter. In short, Micaiah told Ahab that he saw a deceiving spirit enter into the false prophets and that in reality Ahab would die in battle that day. In response Ahab had Micaiah imprisoned, but the word Micaiah spoke came to pass. By the end of the chapter Ahab was dead.

This is how darkness responds to light. It tries to snuff it out, to suppress it, to stifle it. Light makes darkness uncomfortable. Light reveals the uncleanness and the evil. Light exposes the compromise and the corruption. The light simply cannot be allowed to shine. The sinner sleeping in squalor shouts, "Will someone turn off that light?"

The darkness wants to silence the disturbing voice of the prophet, wants to ease its guilty conscience, wants to shut down the unsettling message. And often the best way to do that is by killing the prophetic messenger. That's why so many prophets have been put to death. That's why Jesus used the prophets as an example of those who were persecuted for righteousness (Matt. 5:10–12). That's why He indicted Jerusalem for killing the prophets (Matt. 23:37). That's why a Jewish tradition states that, when called by the Lord, Jeremiah protested, saying, "I cannot prophesy to them [meaning the people of Israel]; what prophet went out to them whom they did not seek to kill?"[2] That's why Jezebel waged war against the prophets of Yahweh, seeking to eradicate them from Israel. With the king on her side, the corrupt priests on her side, the people on her side, and the false prophets on her side, there was only thing opposing her: the true prophetic voice.

In his classic book *The Prophets*, the Jewish philosopher Abraham Joshua Heschel described the unsettling role of the prophets. He wrote, "The prophet's word is a scream in the night. While the world is at ease and asleep, the prophet feels the blast from heaven."[3] Yes, Heschel observed, "The prophet is human, yet he employs notes one octave too high for our ears.... Often his words begin to burn where conscience ends."[4] How the prophet's words do burn!

Leonard Ravenhill, himself a prophetic voice and a broken-hearted man of prayer, also gave classic expression to the prophetic call. He wrote:

> The prophet is violated during his ministry, but he is vindicated by history. He is the villain of today and the hero of tomorrow. He is excommunicated while alive and exalted when dead! He is dishonored with epithets when breathing and honored with epitaphs when dead. He is friendless while living and famous when dead. He is against the establishment in ministry; then he is established as a saint by posterity.[5]

That's why it was inevitable that Jezebel would wage war against Elijah. He was her nemesis, the thorn in her side. It was his head she was after, and at one point she had him on the run. But in the end, it was his words that came to pass, and Jezebel died just as he said.

That's because you can kill the prophet, but you cannot kill his word. You can silence the messenger (at least for a season), but you cannot ultimately silence the message. The word of the Lord will always come to pass. (See Isaiah 40:7–8; 55:10–11.)

DIAGNOSING THE PRESENCE OF THE JEZEBELIAN SPIRIT

When you're feeling sick and you go to a doctor, you tell the physician your symptoms. "Doc, I've been running a fever, coughing, and sneezing. I feel totally wiped out."

The doctor asks, "What about body aches?"

You answer, "My whole body is aching. I feel like every muscle has been stretched."

The doctor replies, "Sounds like the flu."

In the previous chapters we have been examining the symptoms from which America is suffering: idolatry, immorality, abortion, radical feminism, LGBT activism, the war on gender, the rise of witchcraft. A spiritually minded friend might ask, "What about the silencing of the prophets? Is that happening in America today?"

We answer, "Yes, absolutely!"

Our friend replies, "Definitely sounds like Jezebel!"

How is America silencing the prophets? The opposition is coming from both the church and the world, which makes perfect sense if the opposition is spiritual in nature. That's why it can come from multiple places at the same time. Both God's people and the people of the world are resisting the prophetic message.

In the church we have bought into the lie that the gospel message is always and only positive, that God is always happy and jovial, that He's never grieved or angry and never speaks rebuke or correction, that the days of judgment are past, that "negative" prophetic messages were for the Old Testament only. To the prophets the compromised church says, "Give me some candy and some popcorn too. God is throwing a party, and we won't let you spoil our fun."

In the world the message of repentance is branded hateful and the prophetic word dismissed as bigoted. Christians are expected to be nice, and it is not nice to warn sinners about hell or to call them to turn from their wicked ways. "We will have none of your judgmental message," shouts the world to God's prophets.

Sadly, many prophets have gladly accommodated, either retreating into the closet for fear of the consequences or selling out for profit and popularity.[6] Shades of Jezebel once again. She killed and intimidated the true prophets and seduced and supported the false prophets. Only men like Elijah and Micaiah had the gall to stand in her way.

During an interview with conservative journalist Ben Shapiro, Pastor John MacArthur made this simple but penetrating statement: "If you try to develop a kind of Christianity that's inoffensive, it's not Christianity."[7] Well said! The message of salvation through Jesus, the message of the cross, the message of the gospel, brings offense.

When I tweeted Pastor MacArthur's words, they were met with immediate and enthusiastic affirmation.[8] Many in the church *know* something is wrong with our ear-tickling, always-affirming, never-confronting message. That message is *not* the message of the Bible, not the Old Testament and not the New Testament. But it *is* a message that has become very popular today. The narrow way is too confining. Give us that big, broad road!

What did God's people say to the true prophets in Isaiah's day? "Don't tell us what is right. Tell us nice things. Tell us lies. Forget all this gloom. Get off your narrow path. Stop telling us about your 'Holy One of Israel'" (Isa. 30:10–11, NLT). How did Isaiah respond, as inspired by the Spirit? "This is the reply of the Holy One of Israel" (Isa. 30:12, NLT).

Jesus warned His disciples against false prophets, reminding them that the way to eternal life was hard and the gate narrow (Matt. 7:13–20). He made clear that there were serious consequences for neglecting the truth (Matt. 7:21–27).

Paul warned Timothy that "a time is coming when people will no longer listen to sound and wholesome teaching. They will follow their own desires and will look for teachers who will tell them whatever their itching ears want to hear. They will reject the truth and chase after myths" (2 Tim. 4:3–4, NLT).

What was Paul's counsel to Timothy in light of this warning? Simply this: "Preach the word, be ready in season and out of season, reprove, rebuke, and exhort, with all patience and teaching" (2 Tim. 4:2). And he urged Timothy to do it with the utmost sobriety "before God and the Lord Jesus Christ, who will judge the living and the dead at His appearing and His kingdom" (2 Tim. 4:1).

Today in our pulpits there is often so little sobriety, so little fear of God, so little conviction. The preacher must entertain. The sermon must be off the charts. The people must leave smiling. Always. Only.

A strong, loving challenge might turn congregants away. A word of caring rebuke might scare off the big givers. A sobering talk on the judgment to come might be too disturbing. The people might complain, "Pastor, when you talk like that, I don't feel safe!" So instead of confronting, we coddle, and instead of warning, we waffle. Nothing can disrupt the sleep of the slumbering saint!

Like little children, we must be entertained; like toddlers, we must be amused. But this is not how you train an army. This is not how you make disciples. This is not how you raise up world changers. Jezebel is winning here too, by seduction as much as by deception, by appealing to the flesh as much as by suppressing the truth.

As a result we have people who claim to be Bible-believing, Jesus-loving Christians working in almost every imaginable profession (almost nothing seems to be off limits), engaging in virtually every kind of sinful behavior (and I mean openly and proudly), using the foulest language (sometimes from the pulpit, proving that the preacher is not "religious"), having the grimiest attitudes, and showing not the slightest sign of conviction.

It's as if Jesus came to make sinners successful rather than bring them to salvation, as if He called them to celebrate their sinful desires rather than crucify them.

And what happens to those who stand up for holiness, who speak against compromise, who call believers to separation from the pollution of the world? All too often it's a repeat of what happened to Israel in the days of Amos, when the Lord said, "I raised up some of your sons as prophets, and some of your young men as Nazirites. Is it not so, O children of Israel? says the LORD. But you made the Nazirites drink wine, and commanded the prophets, saying, 'Do not prophesy'" (Amos 2:11–12). Do you think I'm exaggerating?

Today the moment believers get really serious about following Jesus, the moment they turn to Him in repentance, the moment they commit to holy living, they are surrounded by "Christian" voices saying, "Don't get too extreme! Be spiritual, not religious! You don't want to get caught up in legalism! Remember, it's all by grace! You need to get rid of that performance mentality!" Once again we are making the Nazirites drink wine. We have forgotten that friendship with the world—meaning sharing in the world's corruption—is enmity with God and that Jesus calls us to go *into* the world when it comes to reaching sinners but come *out of* the world when it comes to the pollution of sin. (See Jacob[9] [James] 4:3; Matthew 28:19; and 2 Corinthians 6:14–7:1.)

I'm reminded again of the Lord's words through Jeremiah: "An appalling and horrible thing has been committed in the land. The prophets prophesy falsely, and the priests rule by their own authority; and My people love to have it so. Yet what will you do in the end?" (Jer. 5:30–31). This applies in particular to so-called "progressive Christians." They deny the absolute authority of Scripture, reinvent God's standards to make them more acceptable to the culture, and present themselves as heroes and saints. It was with them in mind that I tweeted, "Do you want to be a hero to sinners? Tell them they can have Jesus AND their sin at the same time. Do you want to be a help to sinners? Tell them Jesus can forgive them AND set them free from their sins."[10]

But not all God's people want it this way. Far from it. To the contrary, many are sick and tired of a superficial gospel. Many have had it with shallow, feel-good, pep-talk sermons. Many are urging their leaders to stand up and speak out, regardless of cost or consequence, to challenge them with Scripture, to tackle the controversial issues, and to say, "We're not here to play games!"

That's why when I posted Pastor MacArthur's words so many agreed. That's why when we launched our five-minute animated video "Why Don't More Pastors Speak Out?," the responses to the message were overwhelmingly positive, including the feedback from several pastors.[11]

That's why tweets like this receive so much affirmation: "There was a time in America when Christian leaders were expected to speak out against sin. Now, it's considered taboo."[12]

And this: "The gospel of Jesus: If you want to be My disciple, deny yourself, take up the cross, and follow Me. The modern American gospel: God loves you just as you are, so indulge yourself and dream your dreams. God is with you, baby!"[13]

We do not have to be mean-spirited or nasty. God forbid. We do not have to speak with anger or hostility. Perish the thought. We speak with love. We plead. We weep. We admonish with tears.

But we must not bury the uncomfortable truth for fear of offending. We follow Jesus in word, in spirit, and in deed. When we do, the world will treat us the way it treated Him. (See Matthew 10:24; John 15:16–18.) So be it!

We are called to be prophetic, not popular; servants, not superstars; *like* our Savior, not *above* our Savior. As Jesus said, "It is enough for the disciple that he be like his teacher, and the servant like his master. If they have called the master of the house Beelzebub, how much more will they call those of his household?" (Matt. 10:25).

It is true that sinners were drawn to Jesus, and they should be drawn to us too. We should be caring, compassionate, and kind. We should be clothed with love and mercy and goodness; filled with joy and peace; offering healing, restoration, redemption, and new life; bringing a message of hope. Yes, we should shine with the very light of Jesus. Lost sinners will certainly be drawn to that kind of light.

But others will not. They will hate and revile us, harass and persecute us. They will slander and malign us and seek to defame us. They might even assault or arrest or kill us.

So be it! We are called to follow Jesus by life or by death, and the worst the world can do is kill us. (See Matthew 10:18; Philippians 1:21.) That only increases our reward and hastens our promotion to glory. That only spreads our message all the more.

This, then, is how we stand up to Jezebel: overcoming by the blood of the Lamb and by the word of our testimony, and by not loving our lives, even to the point of death (Rev. 12:11).

SHARE GOD'S MESSAGE WITH THE WORLD, NOT JUST THE CHURCH

The world, for its part, is dead set against the message of righteousness, and it has developed an effective method to silence our witness. If we declare that Jesus is the only way, we are branded religious fanatics. If we preach sexual purity, we are called hypocrites. If we speak against abortion, we're accused of provoking the murder of abortion providers. If we say homosexual practice is sinful, we're designated hate-filled homophobes and Nazi bigots. If we denounce witchcraft, we're met with incredulity. "Witchcraft? Seriously?"

This is too much for many believers, who are not prepared for the onslaught against them. Better to stay quiet. Better to keep our convictions to ourselves. After all, we reason, if people think we're fanatics, they won't listen to our message. And with that we sanctify our cowardice and justify our compromise.

And what if we persist and continue to speak out? We will be blacklisted and blackballed. The secular media will shut us out, and the internet will block us out. One group will mock us; another group will ban us. Our reputation will be tarnished, our finances drained, our spirits discouraged.

This, too, is a tactic of Jezebel, and it has worked wonders so far. And so, despite an unprecedented saturation of Christian media in America today—from TV to radio, from books to magazines, from internet to cell phone, from Bible apps to preaching podcasts—in one particular sense the word of the Lord is rare in our land. (See 1 Samuel 3:1 and cross reference with Amos 8:11.)

A VOICE FROM 1944

Three years before he became chaplain of the Senate in 1947, Rev. Peter Marshall preached an urgent message titled "Trial by Fire," which "focused on the spiritual battle portrayed in the Bible between Elijah and the prophets of Baal."[14] As Dr. David R. Reagan related, "Marshall proceeded to express his concern that our nation was getting caught up in the moral drift and confusion that characterized the ancient Israel of the prophet Elijah when that nation became captivated by idolatry and turned its heart away from God."[15]

With passion Marshall said, "Love of power and authority has enslaved the hearts of many Americans. The seeds of racial hate and intolerance have been sown. And we will reap a bitter harvest....Our moral standards have been lowered....And no nation makes progress in a downward direction."[16] He continued:

> We must decide and decide quickly who is chief, whom we will serve. Millions of people in America live in moral fog....Modified immorality on the basis of cleverness guides millions of people. Modified dishonesty within the letter of the law is the practice of millions

more. Surely the time has come, because the hour is late, when we must decide. And the choice before us is plain: Jehovah or Baal. Christ or chaos. Conviction or compromise. Discipline or disintegration.[17]

And then Marshall issued this urgent call for prophetic voices to arise:

I suggest to you that America needs prophets today…who will set before the nation the essential choices….

We need a prophet who will have the ear of America and say to her now, "How long will you halt and stand between two opinions? If the Lord be God, follow Him, but if Baal be God, follow him, and *go to Hell!*"[18]

What would Marshall say us to today, in 2019? Would he even have words to describe his shock and grief? Would he say even more emphatically, and with tears and groans, "I suggest to you that America needs prophets today…who will set before the nation the essential choices"?

Again, to be clear, we have many fine Bible teachers, many encouraging Bible preachers, many solid Bible speakers. But all too often they major only on words of hope and edification, bringing very little conviction to a lost and dying world (or to a compromised church). And, the truth be told, many times they avoid confrontation like the plague. It's too costly to confront sin and too easy to avoid controversy.

If you don't believe me, ask yourself this: When is the last time you heard a message on the coming judgment? When is the last time you heard a strong message on hell? When is the last time you left a service shaken to the core? Now contrast that experience with the teaching of Scripture, where Jesus and Paul and other New Testament writers spoke often about coming judgment and hell. Their messages shake us and stir us. Why the stark contrast between the biblical message and the contemporary message?

As I noted earlier, there was a time in America when Christian leaders were expected to speak out against sin. As a nonbeliever, when you heard evangelist Billy Graham preach, you expected him to call you to repentance. When you saw him as a guest on a TV show, you expected him to talk about the Ten Commandments or sexual purity or hell or the like—but always with incredible grace, kindness, and respect. Today you expect the preacher on TV to sound more like a life coach, more like a motivational speaker, more like a slick salesman.

When you have five minutes, I encourage you to watch this great montage of Billy Graham on secular TV shows, linked here in the endnote.[19] Then ask yourself how many voices we have like this speaking to the secular world. It's even fair to ask, How many voices like this, where they can be found, are even given a platform like this anymore?

Certainly the sins of America will be our undoing unless we turn back to God in repentance. And we, as a nation and as individuals, are responsible for our sins. But the church is responsible as well, and the silence of our prophetic voices makes us complicit.

The spirit of Jezebel working in the church and the world has effectively muzzled our witness, but I sense a holy resistance rising up. Elijah may have run for a moment, but he never backed down again. May we follow his example today.

And may we learn the secret of divine strength out of human weakness. Whereas we in ourselves will always fall short, our frailty is the occasion for God's power to be manifest through us. (See 2 Corinthians 12:9–10.) Our trust is in the Lord!

He is about to rise up, in us and through us. He is about to deal with Jezebel. Are you ready?

CHAPTER 10

JEZEBEL, JEHU, AND DONALD TRUMP

WHILE DOING AN online search for the words *Jezebel* and *feminism*, I discovered an article by Baptist pastor Mike Storti titled "Jezebel—The Original Feminist," in which Pastor Storti came to many of the same conclusions to which I had come. He said, "The spirit of Jezebel, the original feminist, is abounding in America today."[1] Those are almost the exact words I had written before seeing his.

He also made this contemporary application:

> Surely we can see the queen of the radical feminists today with Hillary Clinton. She ruled the U.S. as co-president with her husband for 8 years. Like Jezebel and now, like Athaliah [a Judean queen who killed almost all the male heirs and assumed the throne], she wants to rule over U.S. all by herself....Surely America is in a time of apostasy like the days of Jezebel and Elijah. Surely America is at a crossroads and with no repentance judgment will soon fall.[2]

Is he taking things too far? Is Hillary Clinton a contemporary Jezebel?

Without a doubt she is one of the most powerful and influential female leaders in American history. She was the first lady, a senator, and then Secretary of State under President Obama. And she came very close to being our first female president. She is also an outspoken proponent of women's rights, a strong supporter of Planned Parenthood,[3] a woman firmly committed to the LGBT cause, and someone rumored to be quite ruthless. For better or worse she is one of the leading feminist voices of our generation.

But does that make her a Jezebel? And if she is a Jezebel type of leader, what (or who) does that make Donald Trump?

Obviously, if Hillary Clinton were as wicked and powerful as Queen Jezebel, America would look very different. Christian leaders would be getting butchered in the streets. Church buildings would be closed, Christian websites would be shut down, and believers would be in hiding. Bibles would be confiscated, crosses removed, and Satan (or one of his demonic lackeys) would be recognized publicly as the god of the nation.

So any comparison between Hillary Clinton and Jezebel is just that: a comparison offered to make a point and gain a perspective rather than an actual, factual argument, especially when we speak of Jezebel's violent death. We do not wish this for Hillary Clinton!

It's the same with comparisons between biblical figures and Donald Trump. They are just comparisons, similar to comparing a morally flawed but gifted evangelist to a Samson-type figure or comparing a Christian mother too busy to meet with Jesus to Martha or comparing a zealous but impetuous young leader to Peter.

In that light we can ask again: If Hillary Clinton is likened to a Jezebel-type figure, what does that make Donald Trump? In the Bible, Jezebel met her match with the strong-armed Jehu, and on December 15, 2018, Joel Pollak, an Orthodox Jew and senior editor for Breitbart.com, actually likened Trump to Jehu. He wrote, "In many ways, Trump is reminiscent of the biblical King Jehu, an outsider who was anointed to rule Israel and rid it of corruption.... Jehu also dispatched Ahab's widow, the wicked Queen Jezebel, who had urged her late husband to persecute the prophets."[4]

He continued:

Jehu continued his aggressive campaign to rid the kingdom of corruption. He ordered the execution of seventy of Ahab's sons, and used an ingenious ruse to slaughter all the remaining supporters of Baal, luring them to a temple by promising that he would also worship the idol and then ordering his guards to kill them. Though his methods were unconventional, Jehu earned the support of Jehonadab the son of Rechab, widely respected for his morals.[5]

Trump, then, would be reminiscent of a Jehu-like figure; Trump defeated Hillary Clinton, who was a Jezebel-type figure. Like Jehu, Trump is a rough outsider with unconventional methods, yet a man who gained the support of conservative Evangelicals, people like Mike Pence, who is similar to Jehonadab.

To be sure, Pollak doesn't mention Hillary by name (or direct implication), and his focus was not on Jezebel at all. Rather, his emphasis was that just as Jehu never finished his reforms, Trump too has not finished all of his. And Pollak's main focus was on Trump's failure to build the wall so far.

However, more than one year before Pollak made these comparisons, Messianic Jewish author Jonathan Cahn made them as well in his book *The Paradigm: The Ancient Blueprint That Holds the Mystery of Our Times*.[6] Cahn, however, took them much further, providing more details and potential parallels between Jehu and Donald Trump.

Teaching from his book at a 2018 Bible prophecy conference, Cahn explained how he applied the ancient biblical texts. First, as in Ahab's day, America was at a crossroads during the 2016 elections. Had Hillary Clinton been elected, "it would have sealed the Supreme Court for a generation. It would have ended religious liberty."[7]

Second, "The mystery of Donald Trump is found in Jehu.... Jehu was not a politician, and Donald Trump was not a politician. Jehu was a fighter. Donald Trump is a fighter. Actually, he fights with everybody!"[8]

As Cahn explains:

> Jehu was not a gentleman. Well? Jehu was kind of wild, kind of out of control, and you never knew what he was going to do next. Do I have to say anything? Jehu would come on the national stage suddenly and shake up the status quo, and so, too, with Donald Trump. Jehu would begin a race to the throne of Israel, and Donald Trump will begin a race to the throne of America.
>
> Jehu had not lived a godly life, and neither has Donald Trump. Now this warrior is used, despite himself, for God's purposes in this moment.[9]

As for Jehu being "wild, kind of out of control," Cahn points to 2 Kings 9:20. In that text a watchman reporting on a rider coming to Samaria said that "the driving is like the driving of Jehu the son of Nimshi; for he driveth furiously" (KJV). Other translations render the last words with: "he drives like a maniac" (NIV, NRSV); "he drives like a madman" (CSB); he "drives wildly" (JPS TANAKH); or, "he drives recklessly" (NET). Does this sound familiar?

Third, Cahn writes of the showdown between Jehu the warrior and Jezebel.[10] So, too, with Trump and Hillary. Cahn buttresses his argument with further, detailed parallels, also likening Jehonadab to Pence.

Of course, you must come to your own conclusions about his overall point, namely, that the biblical account of these ancient Israelite kings provides a prophetic paradigm for what is happening today. But one thing is clear to me, and it is clear whether you love Trump or hate him and whether you see him as a gift from God (albeit with many flaws) or as a blight on the nation: *An alpha male leader like Donald Trump will come into direct conflict with the spirit of Jezebel.* It cannot be avoided.

We've seen similar things in Russia, where another alpha male, Vladimir Putin, leads the nation. Some of the most vocal protests against him have come from a feminist group called, not surprisingly, Femen. They are known for their topless demonstrations, which often lead to arrest, and they call themselves "sextremists."

A story from April 2013 reports that when Putin visited a trade fair in Hannover, Germany, on April 8, he was confronted by topless Femen protesters. One of the protesters, Oleksandra Shevchenko, later explained why she and her group targeted the strong-armed Russian leader:

> I don't think we're the only ones who have a problem with Putin. I think the whole planet does. He has done a lot of harm not only to his own Russian citizens but to the whole world. If you are unafraid to express your democratic opinion then it is your duty to come out and say it in his face.
>
> Frankly, your question surprises me because the whole world talks about these problems constantly. Every day they talk about problems regarding Putin in the papers, on the radio. We simply expressed,

laconically, what the whole world wants—for Putin to go or, even better, for him to go screw himself.[11]

There you have it. The "whole planet," the "whole world" has a problem with Putin. (Sound familiar?) Yes, these alpha males, be they good men or bad men, will come into direct conflict with the radical feminists.

As for Donald Trump—to say it once more—when we compare him to Jehu, we are just making a comparison. That doesn't mean that Hillary is (or is not) a Jezebel-type leader, or that Trump is a saint (or a sinner). It doesn't mean he's anointed by God (or not), and it doesn't mean he is (or is not) an abusive misogynist. And it doesn't mean Evangelicals were right (or wrong) in supporting him. (If you'd like to know my perspective on all this, I strongly encourage you to read my book *Donald Trump Is Not My Savior: An Evangelical Leader Speaks His Mind About the Man He Supports as President.*[12])

What all this does mean is this, and it's really hard to deny: the Trump candidacy, followed by the Trump presidency, has brought the worst of radical feminism to the surface. In that sense it has caused Jezebel to come out of the shadows and into the forefront. In that sense Trump is like Jehu, the man who drove "recklessly," the leader who drove like a "madman," like a "maniac."

Just consider some of these disparaging headlines describing President Trump (with my emphasis in italics):

- "Donald Trump Is *Reckless*, Erratic and Incompetent, According to Business Leaders Around the World" (*Newsweek*, June 23, 2017)[13]

- "Majority of Voters Think Trump Is *Reckless*, Poll Says" (*Detroit Free Press*, October 25, 2017)[14]

- "Poll: Majorities Think Trump Is *Reckless*, Profane and Sexist" (*The Hill*, January 28, 2018)[15]

- "Trump's Not a Liar. He's a *Madman*." (*Washington Post*, May 29, 2018)[16]

- "War of Words: Trump, Visionary or *Madman*?" (*The Telegraph*, May 25, 2018)[17]

- "A Virginia Democrat Called Trump a 'Narcissistic *Maniac*.' And He's Not the Liberal in the Race!" (CNN, June 5, 2017)[18]

Trump is a hated man, especially among liberal women. To them he is the ultimate example of a powerful, sexist, abusive male. That's why at a massive women's march immediately after Trump came into office, Madonna openly expressed that she had thought about blowing up the White House. Later that same year, comedian Kathy Griffin held up the bloodied likeness of the president's decapitated head. And month by month witches have gathered to curse and hex him.[19] Shades of the spirit of Jezebel! (Just note this headline from December 21, 2018. It brings together several themes of this book in just a few words: "Witchcraft Moves to the Mainstream in America as Christianity Declines—and Has Trump in Its Sights."[20])

TRUMP HATE

To be sure, there is a lot of female anger toward Trump because of his ugly, sexist past, including both alleged actions and recorded comments.[21] This is understandable, also causing many of these women to ask how any evangelical Christian could vote for him, support him, or work for him.[22] As Claire Cohen wrote in *The Telegraph*, "Fat. Pig. Dog. Slob. Disgusting animal. These are just some of the names that Donald Trump has called women."[23] Even former first lady Michelle Obama "called Trump a 'misogynist' who used birther rhetoric that called into question former President Barack Obama's citizenship to intentionally 'stir up the wingnuts and kooks.'"[24]

Could this be why female celebrities have denounced Trump, with model Chrissy Teigen saying, "Donald Trump is an unwell, evil human being. To the core"?[25] Or, to quote Madonna's sentiments expressed at the 2017 Women's March in Washington, DC, "Yes, I'm angry. Yes, I'm outraged. Yes, I have thought an awful lot about blowing up the White House. But I know that this won't change anything."[26] For these angry women Trump is an easy and justifiable target, which is why he also has an entry in *The Book of Jezebel* under the heading "A Rogue's Gallery of Wretched Misogynists: With its long history, long reach, and impressive staying power, misogyny is truly universal. Yet some individuals cry out for a particular public shaming for their cringe-inducing contributions to the world of women hatred."[27]

Rebecca Traister paints a picture of just how much anti-Trump fury there was at the second Women's March, which took place in 2018. She writes that:

> While taking the subway home from the second annual Women's March, protests conceived in response to the inauguration of President Donald Trump, I scrolled through images on my social media feeds and saw another cascade of wrath....
>
> Some of the women I'd stood near at this 2018 march had held an effigy of Trump's testicles in the air, decorated with a poof of orange hair. Others had depicted him as a pile of excrement. I looked at homemade signs from across the nation, where protests had,

for the second year in a row, taken place not just in New York and Los Angeles and Washington, but in Bangor, Anchorage, Austin, and Shreveport: "[Expletive] you, you [expletive] [expletive]," read one of my favorites. "Feminazis against Actual Nazis," "[Expletive] the Patriarchy," and "Angry Women Will Change the World" were other examples. One woman had cut out a hole for her head and written around it, "Resisting [Expletive] Face."[28]

The truth be told, though, some of the female anger toward Trump—really, it is outright rage—is due to the fact that he has become a pro-life champion, one of the more surprising developments in political memory. His Supreme Court appointees could threaten *Roe v. Wade*, which is one of Jezebel's most carefully guided prizes. And these women will fight and scratch and claw to keep their "right" to abort. When Kavanaugh was being sworn in, some of these women (and some men) literally pounded on the Supreme Court doors, shouting and chanting that Kavanaugh had to go. Jezebel was aroused.[29]

I mentioned earlier that the name Trump occurred 219 times in Rebecca Traister's book on the revolutionary power of female anger. In contrast, Obama was found only 47 times. Hillary occurred only 79 times, while Clinton was found 154 times in the book.[30] That's because Donald Trump has been the trigger point for female outrage, and even though some of the outrage is understandable—just remember how evangelical Christians felt about Bill Clinton—some of it is beyond the pale. The alpha male Trump, the man with the forehead of steel who backs down from no one, the swamp drainer, the bull in the china shop, the chaos president, the divine "wrecking ball"[31]—this man has brought the most extreme elements of radical feminism to the forefront. Jezebel has taken center stage.

To repeat: this applies whether or not you voted for Trump, whether or not you see him as raised up by God as a Cyrus-type figure,[32] and whether or not you see Hillary Clinton as a Jezebel. I'm simply sharing what we can see with our own eyes. A man like Trump brings an angry, even hysterical, radical feminist spirit to the surface.

A January 23, 2017, headline in *The Independent* announced, "Women's March Against Donald Trump Is the Largest Day of Protests in US History, Say Political Scientists."[33] The protesters, who numbered in the millions and filled streets in cities like Los Angeles, New York, and Washington, DC, also drew large numbers in London (reportedly one hundred thousand). Women even gathered to protest in Toronto, Antarctica, and Iraq.[34]

And what was the stated purpose of these marchers? According to the "Guiding Vision and Definition of Principles" document, the Women's March would bring together people from all backgrounds and ages and races on January 21, 2017, "to affirm our shared humanity and pronounce our bold message of resistance and self-determination."[35]

What about specific goals? To be honest, some of the goals seem quite basic and even commendable, as do the goals in other feminist documents and manifestos. All of us should stand *against* police brutality where it exists and *for* people's rights to have to clean water and air and to enjoy public lands. (We can stand for this without embracing environmental extremism.) All of us should agree that a woman should be paid the same as a man for doing the same job.[36]

Other goals, however, reflected specific feminist concerns, like this:

> We firmly declare that LGBTQIA Rights are Human Rights and that it is our obligation to uplift, expand and protect the rights of our gay, lesbian, bi, queer, trans or gender non-conforming brothers, sisters and siblings. This includes access to non-judgmental, comprehensive healthcare with no exceptions or limitations; access to name and gender changes on identity documents; full antidiscrimination protections; access to education, employment, housing and benefits; and an end to police and state violence.[37]

That means the ability to rewrite the sex listed on your birth certificate or driver's license based on your perceived identity. That means your employer could be responsible to pay for your sex-change surgery. That means a man who identifies as a woman (and is clearly a biological male) cannot be refused a job of, say, caring for children in a nursery school. That means a Christian baker could be required to design a cake for a same-sex wedding ceremony.

More fundamentally, it means we must embrace all perceived identities and orientations, including "bi, queer, trans or gender non-conforming."[38] This, too, was very important to the document framers. And notice the LGBTQIA acronym at the beginning of the paragraph, standing for lesbian, gay, bisexual, transgender, queer (or questioning), intersex, and asexual (or allied).

Another stated goal was "reproductive freedom." As the statement read, "We do not accept any federal, state or local rollbacks, cuts or restrictions on our ability to access quality reproductive healthcare services, birth control, HIV/AIDS care and prevention, or medically accurate sexuality education. This means open access to safe, legal, affordable abortion and birth control for all people, regardless of income, location or education."[39] Practically speaking, that means abortion on demand through all nine months of pregnancy, to be provided by the government when needed, and entirely at the discretion of the mother. Are you connecting the dots once again?

And remember: many of the women at these marches were not just committed to their cause; they were seething with anger. Trump was now the whipping post for their hatred. That's because there's a larger spiritual battle as well, and that's why Pastor John Kilpatrick likened the attack on Trump to the conflict between Elijah and Jezebel, saying that, like Elijah, Trump was being attacked by "witchcraft."[40]

Trump is fighting forcefully against abortion. He is actively opposing LGBT extremism. He is standing with and for evangelical Christians, wanting to preserve our liberties and even urging us to come out of our comfy safe spaces and make our voices heard. In that sense, as remarkable as it may seem, he is supporting the prophets of God, as Obadiah did long ago, and saving them from Jezebel.

Trump is also facing down other world powers, as well as taking on radical Islam and standing with Israel. He even moved the US embassy to Jerusalem. This was a massively important act and a courageous one as well—and something that presidents Clinton, Bush, and Obama had been unwilling to do before him.

And that is why Jezebel is so enraged. Her agenda is being threatened. She is confronting her Jehu again.

Ironically, Jehu was committed to abolishing idol worship in Israel—which meant bringing down Jezebel—although it's questionable how much he personally followed Yahweh. The parallels with Trump continue!

But, to repeat, the stage has been set. And that holds true whether you like Trump or not, whether or not you voted for him in the past or would (theoretically) vote for him in the future, or even whether or not he will serve out his first term or be elected to a second term. Trump, like Jehu before him, has brought Jezebel out of the shadows, as the radical feminists rage against him in the streets and the witches curse him in their covens.

It's high time we defeat the spirit of Jezebel and help set these women (and their male allies) free.

CHAPTER 11

HOW TO DEFEAT JEZEBEL IN YOUR PERSONAL LIFE

IT'S TRUE THAT Queen Jezebel was an imposing, dangerous figure. It's true that she decimated the prophets, that she led a nation into idolatry, that she intimidated, and that she seduced. And it's true that she did this because she was not simply operating in her own strength but was demonically empowered as well. This means these same demonic forces operating today are also dangerous, imposing, murderous, seductive, and intimidating. But they are not God! They are not all-powerful and all-wise. There is only one Lord, and His name is Jesus, and *all authority* in heaven and earth is given to Him. (See Matthew 28:18–20.) We ought not to give Jezebel— meaning the satanic powers behind her—more credit than she deserves.

Of course, we do not stand against her lightly or in our own strength. But in Jesus we have no reason to fear. In Jesus *all* satanic powers are under our feet. (See Luke 10:19.)

In 1 Kings 21:23 Elijah prophesied that "the dogs will eat Jezebel by the wall of Jezreel." This was not meant figuratively but literally. Dogs—canines!—devoured this wicked woman. They feasted on her flesh. We read the gory account in 2 Kings:

> When Jehu came to Jezreel, Jezebel heard about it. She put black paint on her eyes, adorned her head, and looked down through the window. As Jehu entered in at the gate, she said, "Is everything all right, Zimri, murderer of his master?"
>
> And he lifted up his face toward the window and said, "Who is on my side? Who?" And two or three eunuchs looked down to him. He said, "Drop her down." So they dropped her down and some of her

blood splattered on the wall and on the horses. Then he trampled her.

Then he entered, ate and drank, and said, "Attend to that cursed woman and bury her, for she is a king's daughter." So they went to bury her, but they found nothing of her except a skull, the feet, and the palms of her hands. They returned and told Jehu, and he said, "This is the word of the LORD, which He spoke by His servant Elijah the Tishbite, saying, 'On the property of Jezreel dogs will eat the flesh of Jezebel. The corpse of Jezebel will be like dung in the field on the property of Jezreel, so that they cannot say, This is Jezebel.'"

—2 KINGS 9:30–37

Notice carefully what happened here. First, Elijah prophesied Jezebel's death, and his words came to pass. It's true that he once ran in fear from her, as we saw in chapter 1, but the words the Lord spoke through him triumphed over her, and she came to a horrific end. Second, Jehu did not fear Jezebel, nor was he seduced by her. She *can* be resisted and rejected. Third, it was eunuchs—in other words, *castrated males*—who threw her to the ground. We'll come to back to this point in the final chapter, but don't overlook it. The castrated ones showed courage and cast this evil woman down. Fourth, in the end she was not noble or powerful or scary at all. She was trampled underfoot and her body eaten by dogs. (Remember that the Jezebel of the New Testament was promised a dreadful fate as well if she refused to repent. See Revelation 2:20–23.)

Now, it's crucial that in the context of this book we remember that we're talking about spiritual forces here, not people. To quote Paul again, "For our fight is not against flesh and blood, but against principalities, against powers, against the rulers of

JEZEBEL'S WAR WITH AMERICA

the darkness of this world, and against spiritual forces of evil in the heavenly places" (Eph. 6:12). We are *not* labeling individuals Jezebel. (Even the questions raised about Hillary Clinton and Jezebel are meant only as a point of comparison.) We are *not* calling for people to be hurt. We are *not* looking for those who oppose us to die horrible deaths. We are *not* looking for dogs to eat their bodies. A thousand times no!

Our battle is spiritual. We're fighting demons. And these demons hate everyone, including those they work through. That means that Jezebel's frontline, human warriors—whoever they might be in our society today—are also prisoners who need liberation. While they are responsible for their actions and for the choices they make, some of them are victims as well. They have been hurt by the church (or others). They are bruised and battered. Behind their anger is pain. Behind their rage is disappointment.

If we view *them* as our enemies, we are missing the point. If we wish evil on *them*, we do not have the heart of the Lord. But if we recognize Satan as our ultimate enemy, then we do spiritual battle with him while blessing those who curse us and loving those who malign us, thereby overcoming evil with good. This is how we overcome! (See Matthew 5:43–48; Romans 12:14, 18–21.) And so, although Jezebel has slain many of God's people through the ages, we need not fear her or cower before her.

In fact, according to many Hebrew scholars, her very name is treated with scorn in the Scriptures. You would only know that if you understood the Hebrew language and the history of the biblical text, but it appears that the name Jezebel is most likely meant as an insult and slight. In order to explain this, let me give you a different example from the Old Testament. The word *baal* in Hebrew (pronounced "bah-ahl") simply means lord, master, owner, or even husband.[1] As such, it could be used as a title for Yahweh. You could call Him *Baali* (pronounced "bah-ah-lee"), meaning my Master, and that would be fine. That's why there are some godly people in the Bible with *baal* in their names.

But *baal* could also refer to the false god Baal, the one whom Elijah challenged on Mount Carmel, the one whom Jezebel worshipped. In that sense it was a dirty word, an ugly word, something not to be spoken. That's why the Lord said through Hosea, "On that day, declares the LORD, you will call Me *Ishi*, 'My Husband,' and will no longer call Me *Baali*, 'My Master.' I will remove the names of the Baals from her mouth, and they will no longer be remembered by their name" (Hos. 2:16–17, my translation).

And what happened to someone from a previous generation who once had *baal* as part of his name, meaning someone from a time when the word could refer to Yahweh? In some cases the later biblical authors changed *baal* to *boshet*, meaning shame (pronounced "boh-shet"). The *baal* word was not to be spoken. That's why Saul's son Esh-Baal, which means man of *baal* (with *baal* referring to Yahweh) is later called Ish-Bosheth, which means man of shame.[2]

What does this have to do with Jezebel, written *izebel* in Hebrew (pronounced "ee-zeh-vel")? Many scholars believe this was not the original form of her name. Instead, they believe, it was something like *izebul* (pronounced "ee-zeh-vool"), meaning "Where is the prince?" (The "prince" here would be Baal.) But leaving her name like that would bring dignity to Baal, so the vowels were changed to read *izebel*, meaning "Where is the dung?"[3] This would also tie in with 2 Kings 9:37, "The corpse of Jezebel will be like dung in the field on the property of Jezreel."[4]

It's true that the spiritual forces we associate with Jezebel are formidable, and they have destroyed many a life. But these forces, like the ancient queen, have been cast down. We need not run and hide. In fact, this is the first major step in overcoming and defeating the spirit of Jezebel in our lives: *we must not be intimidated.*

STEP ONE: FEAR NOT!

Fear paralyzes. Fear suffocates. Fear debilitates. Fear torments. That's why God exhorts us throughout the Scriptures not to fear, not to be terrified, not to be dismayed.

In one of my favorite Old Testament passages God says to Israel, "Do not fear, for I am with you; do not be dismayed, for I am your God. I will strengthen you, I will help you, yes, I will uphold you with My righteous right hand" (Isa. 41:10). If we know that God is with us and for us, how can we fear? Fear whom? Fear what? Surely our God is greater!

Jesus also encouraged His disciples with similar words, saying, "Do not be afraid, little flock, for it is your Father's good pleasure to give you the kingdom" (Luke 12:32). And, "Peace I leave with you. My peace I give to you. Not as the world gives do I give to you. Let not your heart be troubled, neither let it be afraid" (John 14:27). Jesus did not speak these words in vain. In Him there is zero reason for fear. Ever.

At one time the boxer Mike Tyson was one of the most intimidating figures in sports, and many of his opponents were defeated before the fight ever started. He could look into their eyes and see the fear, and the moment he did, he knew he won. He was a bully, and other fighters feared him for good reason. But then another fighter, Evander Holyfield, refused to be bullied by the bully, and he defeated Tyson not once, but twice.

Many believers are so afraid of Jezebel, so intimidated by her, so in awe of her demonic power, that they forget who they are in Jesus. They are so focused on her—meaning on the demonic forces we have described in this book—that they have taken their eyes off the Lord. That's why I often say that my focus is not on a big, bad devil but on a glorious, all-powerful God. He alone is the King, and to Him alone will every knee bow and every tongue confess. Let's keep our eyes where they belong, on the Lord Jesus.

We can debate the exact nature of this Jezebelian spirit. Is it a principality? Is it just a powerful demon? Is it a coalition of demonic forces that work together? However you understand it, the bottom line is that this demonic power is part of Satan's army, which means it is (or they are) under his command. Yet *he*—the devil himself—has been defeated by Jesus at the cross. As the Word declares, "For this purpose the Son of God was revealed, that He might destroy the works of the devil" (1 John 3:8).

The devil has been vanquished by the cross and resurrection of Jesus, and in Jesus we have authority over Satan. Why, then, should we be intimidated by one of the devil's underlings?

STEP TWO: GIVE NO PLACE TO JEZEBEL IN YOUR LIFE!

If we are to walk in God's authority, if we are to hide ourselves in Jesus, we cannot play games with Jezebel, in particular when it comes to sexual sin. She is still a seductress, and if she can seduce us, she can drain of us confidence, of boldness, of assurance, of faith.

Really now, how can you preach with power against sin when you're living in sin? How can you resist the devil in faith when you're welcoming him into your heart and your home?

Jezebel not only emasculates by intimidation. She also emasculates by seduction.

To every woman reading this book, I urge you to be vigilant. Perhaps you struggle with porn or sexual immorality, just as many guys do. If so, when I speak to them about porn in a moment, you can listen in as well. But for now let me urge you not to be conformed to her ways. Don't get caught up with the spirit of the age. You do not need to have a perfect body. You do not need to compete with that airbrushed model on the screen. Your identity is not tied up with being sexually attractive to every man who passes by. There is a beauty to modesty, a glory that accompanies purity.

But perhaps these temptations of the flesh are not your issue. Perhaps you're not happy with your marriage. It's lacking romance, lacking sizzle. And your husband is preoccupied with work, life, and sports. So you take refuge in the fantasy of romance novels, and before long you're engaging in fantasies of your own that do not involve your husband. Careful! Jezebel wants to destroy you and your marriage. Don't give her an inch. Better to have a less than ideal marriage—although it doesn't have to stay that way—than to fall into adultery.

To every man reading this book, I urge you to be vigilant. Sexual temptation is everywhere around us, though you don't need me to tell you that. Just today I must have deleted a dozen or more sexually themed emails from my junk folder. (I imagine that's what they were; I just saw the subject lines, from Asian girls or Russian girls or whoever wanting to meet me. I bet they want to meet you too!) Porn is so available, so accessible—and so destructive. It will dull you and deaden you. It could even depress you and destroy you. Jezebel is not playing games.

If you are struggling here, make a decision to get help. You *can* be set free. You *can* break the porn addiction. You *can* be a former sex addict. I list some good resources in the endnotes,[5] so check them out and take the first big step. And don't let Satan condemn you either! Lots of men struggle here, including plenty of believers and even leaders. The blood of Jesus cleanses, the Holy Spirit delivers, and the Father reaches down to help.

But I urge you again: be vigilant. Porn has led to many a divorce. Porn has desensitized many a conscience. Porn has opened the door to real-life hookups instead of just chat rooms. And even without porn the temptation to commit fornication or adultery is as old as the human race.

One thing, though, should be clear to you by now: Jezebel is just plain evil, and her goal is your destruction. When you open the door through pornography, you're opening the front door of your soul and inviting her in. Don't do it!

STEP THREE: PUT ON THAT DIVINE ARMOR!

It's clear that we can't fight demonic powers, let alone Satan himself, in our own strength. The devil is incredibly crafty, devious, cunning, enticing, murderous, destructive, heartless, and ruthless—just to name a few of his negative attributes. As human beings we cannot fathom how evil he is, and he has a massive army of mayhem at his disposal. You do not want to take him on lightly, and I see no reason to call him out or challenge his forces, as in "Devil, let's see what you've got!" or "Jezebel, bring it on!" But that doesn't mean we don't take our stand. That doesn't mean we don't go on the attack. We just do it clothed with the armor of God, as described in Ephesians 6:10–18.

There are some really good studies on this subject, and you might want to look into them.[6] Here I only want to make one simple point, but it's a point that can change your perspective and even your life. *The armor we put on is God's own armor.* That's right. It's the same armor He wears, spiritually and metaphorically speaking. We are truly clothed with His power. We really do fight with His weapons. That's why it's called "the armor of God," and that's why "the sword of the Spirit" is "the word of God" (Eph. 6:17). So it's not just the armor He gives us. It's the armor He Himself wears, again, spiritually speaking, and the weapons with which He fights. Let me prove it to you from the Bible.

In Ephesians 6:14 Paul tells us to put on the "breastplate of righteousness," but what does he mean by that? Does he mean we cover our hearts with the knowledge that we are righteous? Perhaps there's some truth to that, but is that everything Paul is saying?

In Ephesians 6:17 he urges us to put on the "helmet of salvation," but what exactly does that mean? Does it mean "put a helmet over your mind, reminding yourself that you are saved"? Certainly that's not a bad idea, and we must renew our minds with the Word of God. And Paul urges us in 1 Thessalonians 5:8 to put on "as a helmet, the hope of salvation."

But these terms mean something even more specific in Ephesians 6, and we find both of them used earlier in the Scriptures in Isaiah 59:17. The surprise, though, is that *God Himself* puts these on. As the text states, "For He put on righteousness as a breastplate and a helmet of salvation on His head; He put on the garments of vengeance for clothing and was clad with zeal as a cloak."[7]

Now, do you think the Lord puts on a breastplate to remind Himself He is righteous? Obviously not. Do you think He wears a helmet to remind Himself that He is saved? Hardly! What, then, do the images convey? And is there another way the Hebrew could be translated? I love this rendering from the Jewish Publication Society version: "He donned victory like a coat of mail, with a helmet of triumph on His head; He clothed Himself with garments of retribution, wrapped himself in zeal as in a robe." Now we're talking!

Even if we retain the word *righteousness* rather than *victory*, the overall message is clear: "According to Ephesians 6 believers need to be armed with God's own righteousness if they are to be protected against the blows and arrows of their spiritual enemies."[8] You stand in the victory of God, wearing His very righteousness as a breastplate. Now you're ready for battle!

What about the helmet? The Hebrew word for *salvation* does not simply emphasize being saved; it speaks also of triumph. The Savior is the victor! The Deliverer is the triumphant One! Here, as one commentator notes, "he gives his helmet to believers for their protection."[9] You can feel pretty safe wearing a helmet like this! It is the helmet of God's victory, the helmet of spiritual triumph, the helmet of the overcomer. Put that helmet on!

It's as if you're in a movie and you have discovered the superhero's special suit or secret weapon. When you put on that suit or use that weapon, you have superpowers too. But this is not a movie, nor is it some silly suit or mythical weapon. This is reality. We put on God's own armor. We fight with His strength. Forward, in Jesus' name!

STEP FOUR: SEAL IT WITH THE JOY OF THE LORD!

Finally, to seal the deal, the joy of the Lord is essential, and the reason for this is simple. Jezebel thrives in an atmosphere of fear and intimidation, and *fear always points to something bad in the future.* Did you ever realize that?

If you're sitting home and suddenly feel fearful, it's because you think something bad is going to happen. A family member is about to get sick. A friend is going to get into an accident. A murderer is going to break into your house. The roof is going to collapse. Fear torments you with negative thoughts about the future. You think to yourself, "Oh no. Everyone is going to find out about that sin I committed last year." Or, "That mark on my skin is cancerous. I know it. I'm going to die." Or, "I'll never be able to get pregnant," or, "I won't be able to bring that baby to full term. I'm going to have another miscarriage," or, "My baby will be born with a serious defect."

Fear, fear, fear. And how do you fight it? How do you fight lies when you can't prove they are lies? That's where you need the confidence of God, and there's no better place to get that confidence than in the joy of the Lord. As the Word declares, in His presence is fullness of joy, and the joy of the Lord is our strength! (See Psalm 16:11 and Nehemiah 8:10.)

The night before Thanksgiving in 2018 I had some free time while Nancy and our daughters prepared for the big family day, so I put on my earphones to listen to some joyful praise music. As I did, almost instantly I was hit with the joy of the Lord—and I mean hit. My whole being was flooded with an inexpressible and glorious joy (see 1 Peter 1:8), and all I could do was jump and dance and raise my hands and rejoice and smile. I was so full of joy that I wanted to jump out of my body in praise. Glory to God!

And what thoughts flooded my mind? First was the amazing goodness of the Lord. How merciful He has been to me! How faithful! How loving! Second was this: Everything is going to be all right! All your dreams will come true! It's all real!

You say, "But isn't that always your mindset? Aren't you a man of faith?"

Actually, that *is* my normal mindset, and I *am* a man of faith. But this took things to a whole new level. It brought me into a heavenly perspective, as if I were looking *down* on all the powers and people against me. (In fact, I also felt deep pity for those who opposed me. I was struck by just how much they were on the wrong side.) The victory was assured! It's as if I were looking *back* at the trials and tests. They were all behind me, and I was enjoying the heavenly reward. It felt so real, as it might feel if during a time of financial crisis in your life God showed you a picture of your future in which you were living in a beautiful house and giving away millions for the gospel. Everything is going to be all right!

That's when it struck me so clearly: *the joy of the Lord drives out fear, which is always prophesying failure to you.* (Recently, when a dental assistant asked me if I wanted laughing gas along with Novocain before having my tooth pulled, I replied, "The joy of the Lord is better than laughing gas!")

Jezebel's fear says, "You're coming down!" God's joy says, "You're going to make it!"

Jezebel's fear says, "You will most certainly fail and fall!" God's joy says, "I'm with you, and I will keep you strong to the end!"

Jezebel's fear lies to you about your future, promising you horror and dread and shame. God's joy gives you a glimpse of what He has in store for you, and it is glorious beyond words.

Jezebel's fear reminds you of your sins, telling you there's no way back, no forgiveness, no restoration. God's joy shows you the cross and resurrection and tells you you're forgiven and made new in His Son.

God's joy, which is based on God's truth, drives out Jezebel's fears, which are empowered by her lies. But when we listen to her lies, we fall prey to her fears and open to the door to her power.

When we worship the Lord and focus on His goodness, when we praise Him for who He is and what He has done, we take hold of His truth, we shut the door on the lies (as in "Devil, you lose!"), and we are filled with hope, confidence, and faith.

Perfect love casts out fear (1 John 4:18), and in that perfect love comes overflowing, holy, life-giving joy. Jezebel cannot live in an atmosphere like this. Joy will chase her out!

CHAPTER 12

HOW TO DEFEAT JEZEBEL ON A NATIONAL LEVEL

IT'S EASY TO get mad at people, at *them*. The media is not fair. The courts are biased. The schools are brainwashing our kids. The porn industry is evil. Hollywood is pumping out trash. The internet giants are anti-Christian. LGBT activists are taking away our rights.

We all have our list of grievances. We all have our pet peeves. And many of them are quite valid. We *do* have reason to be grieved, and people *are* responsible for their actions. At the same time, our real enemies are spiritual. Our biggest battle is with satanic powers. And that is a major reason I have written this book: to help us connect the dots. To help us see that there is a related, integrated coalition of demonic forces attacking our nation, and those forces have the characteristics of Jezebel.

How, then, do we defeat Jezebel on a national level? Obviously, if we want to help others, we must get our own houses in order. As some of us said years ago during court battles over the public display of the Ten Commandments, the biggest problem is not that we've taken these commandments out of our schools; it's that we removed them first from our hearts and homes. That's why in the last chapter we laid out some practical strategies for defeating Jezebel in our personal lives. First we get our own houses in order. Then we turn to the nation.

STEP ONE: WE MUST GIVE OURSELVES TO PRAYER!

Now that we have established that our greatest battle is spiritual, that some of the biggest problems we face as a nation are interrelated, we understand how we must wage war. It begins on our knees. It begins in the prayer room and at the prayer meeting. It begins with fasting, with intercession, with prevailing prayer and persevering prayer, with fervent prayer and focused prayer. It begins with crying out—real, genuine, crying out to our Father—and with faith-filled rebuking of the enemy.

When we pray like this, we *will* see results. When we take hold of God's promises, when we reverently hold Him to His Word (He loves when we do that), when we exercise our spiritual authority, things will happen. They must!

That doesn't mean that we will see national (or even local) transformation in a day, a week, a month, or even a year. It does mean that God will "avenge His own elect…who cry day and night to Him" (Luke 18:7). It does mean that prayer changes things. It does mean that our heavenly Father hears and answers prayer.

Unfortunately, while the condition of the nation is desperate, the attitude of God's people is not. So many of us are complacent when it comes to today's spiritual and moral crisis. (Hopefully, if you started this book with a complacent attitude, you are complacent no more!) We need some holy desperation. We need some intensity, some passion. God responds to those who seek Him earnestly, who cry out from the heart. It is written in His Word, so it will be!

Even now this cry rises from my heart: *Father, we ask You to dismantle Jezebel's strongholds! We cry out to You to bring down everything that exalts itself against You! Expose the evil, we pray. Reveal the satanic strategies. Set the captives free! And Father, in the name of Jesus we take authority over the enemy and declare that America does not belong to him, that he is not the Lord, and that nothing can stop the advance of Your kingdom!*

The Lord will lead you as you pray, and there are many other steps we must take. But we will never graduate from the school of prayer. Our battle is spiritual. The dots are connected. Our first weapon is always prayer.

Of course, it's easy to get discouraged since major change does not happen overnight, and it seems like Christians are always having prayer meetings and calling for seasons of fasting and prayer. But the reality is that very few really respond (in terms of the whole body). Very few really cry out persistently. Consequently, if more of us took the Lord's invitation to ask and believe, if more of us persevered, we would see glorious results.

It is reported that in 1905 during the Welsh Revival, someone asked Evan Roberts, "What is the secret of revival?" He replied, "There is no secret. It is only, 'Ask, and receive.'"[1]

STEP TWO: THE PROPHETS MUST SPEAK!

It was one thing to be silenced during the days of Jezebel. She was literally killing the prophets, and I don't imagine her henchmen cared about how they went about their bloody business. This was brutal work, and the suffering was acute. If you did stand up and speak out, you could be dead within the hour, if not on the spot.

That's why godly Obadiah worked behind the scenes to take two groups of fifty prophets and hide them in caves, where he provided for them. To venture out of those caves meant a very probable death. To venture out and speak meant a certain death.[2]

Again, this does not excuse the silence of the prophets, and not all were silent. Elijah took his stand at the risk of his own life. But at least it's understandable why they were on the run. To speak was to be killed. Guaranteed. This will certainly shut some mouths.

But today in America who is putting a gun to our heads or a knife to our throats? (I mean this literally.) Who is threatening us with death if we speak? And yet so many of us are silent.

So many have retreated. So many have given way to a spirit of fear. So many have made a bargain with the devil, basically saying, "I won't bother you if you don't bother me. I'll stay in my nice, safe, popular lane, and you stay away from my family." I'm talking about preachers. About pastors. About prophets. I'm talking about local leaders and national leaders.

Thank God for those with holy backbone. Thank God for those who are willing to pay the price to take a stand. Thank God for those who speak the truth in love, who walk in courage, who don't back down. From the heart I thank God for each of you, and I applaud you in the Lord. Stay strong, my friends! We need you on the front lines.

But all too many are in self-imposed spiritual exile. All too many have made a calculated decision to stay out of the fray. All too many have put outward success before inward obedience. All too many have taken the path of least resistance. This cannot continue!

When working on my 2017 book *Saving a Sick America*, I felt especially stirred when writing the chapter titled "Restoring Thunder to Our Pulpits." I began that chapter with this quote from Charles Finney, published December 4, 1873. And although much has changed in America from his day until ours, his words remain piercing and relevant. He said:

> Brethren, our preaching will bear its legitimate fruits. If immorality prevails in the land, the fault is ours in a great degree. If there is a decay of conscience, the pulpit is responsible for it. If the public press lacks moral discrimination, the pulpit is responsible for it. If the church is degenerate and worldly, the pulpit is responsible for it. If the world loses its interest in religion, the pulpit is responsible for it. If Satan rules in

our halls of legislation, the pulpit is responsible for it. If our politics become so corrupt that the very foundations of our government are ready to fall away, the pulpit is responsible for it. Let us not ignore this fact, my dear brethren; but let us lay it to heart, and be thoroughly awake to our responsibility in respect to the morals of this nation.[3]

It's time we arise and speak! It's time we overcome the fear of rejection, the fear of conflict, and the fear of loss, and with hearts aflame and minds ablaze with truth and love and righteousness and compassion, it's time we speak to our nation.

"But I have no national platform!" some will say. "I pastor a small congregation out in the backwoods of America." Or, "I only have thirty followers on Instagram." Or, "I'm not on the radio or TV, and I don't even know how to upload a video to YouTube."

That may be true, but:

1. You do have a sphere of influence, be it in your local congregation, your family and circle of friends, the people you reach online, or the people you work with. You *are* reaching people. The question is how and with what message you are reaching them.

2. If you're faithful with the little, God will give you more, either in numbers or influence, or both. Don't worry about speaking to millions today. Speak to those you can, be it to ten, a hundred, a thousand, or ten thousand.

3. If all of us used the platforms we *do* have, the whole nation would be impacted overnight. The

church is the greatest grassroots movement there is, with hundreds of thousands of spiritually connected branches throughout the land.

You say, "But I don't know what to say. What message am I to bring?"

How about a holy wake-up call? How about using the words of Jesus? How about educating your people on the issues? If you just go through what we've laid out in this book, using the books and articles we cite to further inform you, and then share that information with your people, they too will be equipped. They are looking for answers!

In late 2018 one of my colleagues, Tom Gilson, posted an urgent message on The Stream calling for believers to wake up to the moral crisis at hand. He wrote:

> Western society is rapidly moving toward totalitarianism. I never would have thought it possible—yet it's happening. Christianity in particular is under attack, at risk like never before in our part of the world. I'm not new to these issues, but a recent *National Review* article by John Daniel Davidson was still a kick in the gut for me. We must wake up. We must rouse ourselves to action.
>
> From Davidson's article: Peter Vlaming, a teacher at a small-town Virginia school, was fired recently for "misgendering" a trans person. [In other words, for saying that in good conscience before God he could not refer to a biological female as male if the child identified as transgender.] He sought a compromise answer, but trans activists insisted on a totalitarian

one. They demanded total obedience to their standards. The board caved to them.

Davidson explains, "School officials, likely terrified of what would happen to them if they didn't deliver Vlaming's head on a platter to this student and her family, were only too willing to ruin the man."[4]

Yes, this is happening in America, and it's just one of many shocking examples that could be offered. *They are happening because we are silent.* They are happening because "This is none of my business." They are happening because we have lost our social conscience. They are happening because Jezebel has seduced us or intimidated us.

I say enough is enough. I say it's time to stand and speak. Do you agree?

Gilson offered six practical strategies for action. Note carefully his first three:

> *First: Tell the whole truth.* Don't hold back! Let your congregation know how we're at risk. *All of us* are at risk. Learn what's going on. Study the cultural situation. Read *The Stream*, for starters. However you do it, *please*: Wake up your people!
>
> *Second: Again, tell the whole truth.* God is still God. His Word is still His Word, and that includes His moral instruction. He hasn't changed His mind on any of it. He's also still our Lord and Savior, and we're still in His good hands—no matter what.
>
> *Third: Remind them Jesus still lives, and we must live for Him, no matter what.* That includes repentance in many ways for many of us, and standing with all that His Word teaches, for *all* of us. To suffer for Him—if

necessary—is worth it. We must not fall away from the
only One who saves.[5]

Before 2004 I knew very little about gay activism. I knew
very little about some of the radical strategies. I knew little
about the very real struggles Christians with same-sex attraction experience. I didn't come out of homosexuality. That was
not my background. And God had called me to other areas
of ministry. Plus my PhD was in Near Eastern languages and
literatures. Why in the world would the Lord call *me* to get
involved with LGBT issues? And weren't there enough fine
ministries and organizations out there already? People like
Focus on the Family founder James Dobson, Prison Fellowship
founder Chuck Colson, and Family Research Council president Tony Perkins were already doing a great job. Why me?

What I quickly realized was that this issue—that of LGBT
activism and the response of the church—is the great moral
challenge of our era. We already knew abortion was wrong;
we have just been slow to take strong action. We already knew
pornography was a growing problem; we were just battling it
ourselves. But dealing with LGBT issues? Who was ready for
this? Yet on every front we were being challenged and confronted, from our children's schools to our places of business
and from the halls of justice to the halls of our denominational headquarters.

So I studied and learned. I met with people to hear their
stories in order to develop compassion and understanding. I
got involved and on the front lines, and I did it by the calling
of the Lord. That means I can be a resource now for you. You
don't have to do all the hard work and digging. It's been done
for you by me and by many before me, people from whom I
learned and on whom I leaned.

You can do the same for your flock and for all those you touch. Get equipped, and then equip them. Be an influencer rather than being influenced. Together, with God's help, we can do this!

Whatever area you're burdened in, or wherever Jezebel is most at work in your sphere, get with the Lord, get educated, and then get out and educate and equip others. On my website, AskDrBrown.org, we have a digital library with *thousands* of free resources—articles, videos, and radio broadcasts. Many of these resources are devoted to the most difficult issues of our day, and they are there waiting for you. Dive in, learn, grow, and then share![6]

We're even producing a series of short animated videos called "Consider This" that addresses many of the most difficult and controversial subjects.[7] In just five or six minutes you'll be on your way to better understanding. Or you can simply share these videos with others or show them to your church. Why not?[8]

And to all my colleagues with national platforms: America needs your voice now more than ever. Take up the cross and follow Jesus afresh. Don't let ratings and reviews dictate your choices. Get a fresh message from heaven, raise your voice, and speak. The prophets must no longer be silenced!

As I write these words, Wang Yi, pastor of Early Rain Covenant Church in Chengdu, Sichuan, is imprisoned in China. Despite the government's recent crackdown on Christianity, and knowing full well the consequences of his actions, he said in a sermon on September 9, 2018, that if Xi Jinping, the president of China, "does not repent he will perish!" Yes, he proclaimed, "This government that he is leading has sinned greatly against God. For it is persecuting the church of the Lord Jesus Christ. And if he does not repent he will perish!"[9]

It takes boldness to speak like that, especially knowing the intense suffering he could endure for his message, yet he spoke out just the same. He said:

> When we are not being persecuted, we spread the gospel. And when persecution comes, we continue spreading the gospel....If we are talking about a president, we declare he is a sinner. And if we are talking about a general secretary, we still declare that he is a sinner. We believe we have the responsibility to tell Xi Jinping that he is a sinner.[10]

Closer to home, in Canada, Professor Jordan Peterson made clear that he would resist any government attempts to limit his speech (or, more specifically, to force him to use terms and expressions with which he differed; the issue had to do with referring to transgender-identified people with the pronouns of their choice under penalty of law). He said, "If they fine me, I won't pay it. If they put me in jail, I'll go on a hunger strike. I'm not doing this. And that's that. I'm not using the words that other people require me to use. Especially if they're made up by radical left-wing ideologues."[11]

And what has happened to Professor Peterson as a result of his stand? Is he in prison? Has he been fired from his job? To the contrary, he has become an internet sensation, a best-selling author, a cultural icon, and the archenemy of radical feminism.[12] He has even been labeled "the most influential public intellectual in the Western world right now."[13] There's a lesson here for us!

STEP THREE: PUSH BACK!

It's not just a matter of leaders speaking up. The body must stand together and push back against radical activism, the kind of activism that makes way for stories like this:

> On December 1 [2018], an 11-year-old boy dressed in drag danced on stage in a sexual manner at a gay bar in Brooklyn, NY, called 3 Dollar Bill. The child, Desmond Napoles, was dressed as a Gwen Stefani-lookalike—full drag make up, a blonde wig, and crop top included—as he bounced around onstage to No Doubt's "Just a Girl" and collected dollar bills from male adults viewing the number.[14]

Yes, we must push back against the kind of activism that opened the door for library announcements like this, for parents of children ages two to six: "Learn about someone new! Local drag queens present stories and encourage us all to embrace our uniqueness."[15]

I'm talking about the kind of activism that made possible a story like this one by Todd Starnes: "Parents are furious after children as young as 5-years-old were exposed to an erotic drag show performance at what was supposed to be a school district talent show."[16] How bad was it? Starnes writes: "The *New York Daily News* described the lewd performance as 'complete with gyrations, tongue gymnastics and a flashed G-string.'" I'm not making this up. Really, it's too sick to make up.[17]

He continues: "The May 25th performance shocked and enraged parents who could not believe the school district would allow a grown man to spread his legs and display his crotch to wide-eyed children." Starnes noted that one parent "filmed the seven-minute routine on her cell phone and provided me with a copy. It's jaw-dropping, folks. And when the drag queen dropped to the floor and began writhing in a sexually-suggestive manner, the auditorium erupted."[18] Did you get that? This perverse performance was seven minutes long. In front of five-year-olds. I'm shocked some parents didn't walk right up to the stage and shut the whole thing down.

How in the world did something like this happen in America in the year 2017? The answer is simple: most of the church in America—and I'm talking about Evangelicals and born-again believers, not just nominal Christians—ignored the hand-writing on the wall. We ignored the warnings from those who were speaking up. We didn't want to seem intolerant. We didn't listen when our kids came home from school with some very strange reports. Plus we're too busy. Who has time to go to a local school board meeting? Who has time to examine all our children's textbooks?

Well, those excuses don't stand up anymore, and little by little, in state after state, believers are pushing back. They're respectfully telling their employers they cannot comply with an unfair policy. They're going with their children to meet with school administrators to say with grace but with firmness, "This is not going to happen on my watch." They're taking a stand even when it costs them their jobs, then taking the case to court with the help of Christian legal organizations and even winning at the Supreme Court level.[19]

A friend of the family contacted me recently to tell me that her fifteen-year-old daughter now identifies as a boy and wants to be recognized as such. And her school is encouraging her decision. This concerned mom, together with her husband, went to the school and met with a counselor who informed them that the school was about to announce that their daughter was a boy and to refer to him by a boy's name. They were absolutely shocked.

She explained:

> The school was giving her info, if we were not accepting of her new identity, that she should get us to sign away our rights as a parent and she could live in a group home with other children who have been kicked out of their homes, who may also be gay (which she says she is bi). Can you believe she was getting counsel like that at 15 years old?? That she would live in a home where children have been massively sexually abused, or from violent homes, etc. All this was supposed to "go down" today without our knowledge!!!

This is their daughter, and the school was about to make this decision for her *without parental consent or knowledge*. This is beyond wrong. This is absolutely outrageous. You can be sure these parents pushed back hard, and for the moment the school has backed down.

There's an organization that started in Massachusetts that is now going nationwide and worldwide. It's called MassResistance, and it has been pushing back against radical activism since 1995 (and paying quite a price along the way).[20] Not all of its members or leaders are Christians, and not all Christians would be comfortable with everything they do. (I don't mean they are violent. Never! I mean they don't mind shouting loudly if that's the only way to be heard.) But this much is clear: They're getting results because they're making an effort. They're getting the truth out to local school communities. They're exposing the darkness. And they're winning hearts and minds.

A story on their website dated December 12, 2018, declares:

> MassResistance fight against 'Drag Queen Story Hour'
> targeting children goes national
> Across the country outraged parents and activists
> have begun contacting us for help
> Public officials and media also taking notice and
> reacting
> Here's our report on New York, Alaska, and
> Michigan. More to come![21]

And they're not afraid to distribute real-life pictures from these events.[22] Parents need to know!

If you're not sure what to do in your community or school or place of business, reach out to MassResistance, or reach out to one of the legal organizations that defend religious liberty, like the Alliance Defending Freedom (ADF), Liberty Counsel, First Liberty Institute, or the Pacific Justice Institute. You are not alone!

In November 2016, shortly before he became famous in the United States, I interviewed Jordan Peterson.[23] A psychology professor, he had studied the tactics of totalitarianism for many years, and he was not about to bow down to the thought police who enforced politically correct speech. (In this case being forced to identify students by the pronoun of their choice, regardless of their biological sex.)

At that time, I knew little of Professor Peterson's background, and for the interview I expected to speak with someone who felt like a victim and was hurting. After all, he was singled out for stinging criticism online and in Canadian media, and he told me at the time that his own university said it would not stand with him legally.[24] To my pleasant surprise, he didn't sound like a victim at all. No sob story from him!

The man was a fighter. He pushed back. And now, as I previously mentioned, he is an internet superstar with a massive following, best-selling books, and many powerful video clips where he takes down liberal opposition.[25] And he's still teaching at his university. It's time to push back!

STEP FOUR: LET'S LEARN WHAT WE CAN FROM PRESIDENT TRUMP

We can also learn from President Trump when it comes to taking a stand and pushing back, although quite obviously there are many things we cannot and should not learn from him. We don't need to call people debasing names or label them dogs or use profane speech. And even more obviously, we have no desire to emulate the president's carnal past, from adulterous affairs to building casinos. That is obviously not what I'm saying. But there *are* things we can learn from President Trump that are especially effective when dealing with Jezebel.

One lesson, which is particularly important for Christian leaders, is this: *don't avoid confrontation.* We often try so hard to be nice. At all costs we do not want to offend. But sometimes confrontation is necessary, and there are scores of biblical examples for this. Nathan the prophet confronted King David (2 Sam. 12). Paul confronted Peter (Gal. 2). Proverbs even says, "Better is open rebuke than hidden love" (27:5, ESV). And the New Testament calls us to "speak the truth in love" (Eph. 4:15, NLT).

A second lesson is this: *don't be a slave of public opinion.* It's becoming increasingly clear that Trump controls the media much more than the media controls Trump. This is not to say he doesn't care about polling and negative reports. Nor is this to say we should turn a deaf ear to the voices of others. Shepherds need to be attentive to their sheep.

But all too often as Christian leaders we are more concerned with human opinion than divine opinion, more wanting to please other people than to please the Lord. And all too often we tell people what they want to hear rather than what they need to hear. This not only hurts the flock; it hurts us as well. Let us take heed to these words of Dr. Martin Luther King, "The ultimate measure of a man is not where he stands in moments of comfort and convenience but where he stands at times of challenge and controversy."[26]

A third lesson is this: *don't be afraid to ride out the storm.* Some would call this stubbornness, others conviction, others foolishness. But it's clear that Trump is not afraid to take a stand, take some hits (as in day and night media bombardment), and hold to his guns, believing that over time he will be proven right.[27] In our case we are absolutely assured of the final triumph of the kingdom of God. We also know that societies, like individuals, reap what they sow. That means that over time the truth of our message will rise to the surface as the folly of the world's wisdom and ways is exposed.

In light of that final, glorious triumph when Jesus returns, Pastor Mike Hayes exhorts us to stand:

> So I encourage you—until that glorious day of total renewal—FIGHT ON! We may lose some battles but we will win the war. Sometimes weary, sometimes lonely, sometimes wounded, but always believing, we anticipate that glorious day. It may be our generation or the next, but we never quit working, restoring, believing, and behaving like we know that eventually we will win. Never forget the awesome privilege it is to

be a small part of the greatest cause that we could ever
be involved in helping accomplish![28]

There's an internet article by Evan Sayet, himself a former
liberal, which has been shared over 135,000 times and posted
on numerous websites. It's simply called "He Fights," and it
refers, not surprisingly, to Trump.[29] While it's important to
read the article through a New Testament filter (considering,
especially, passages like 1 Peter 2:23, which reminds us that we
don't revile those who revile us), it is worth a read.

STEP FIVE: THE CASTRATED MALES
MUST REGAIN THEIR MANHOOD

Last, and certainly not least, we need to revisit the account of
Jezebel's death, although I repeat, we are making a *spiritual
application*. When it comes to those who oppose us, we bless
those who curse us and we pray for those who despitefully use
us, leaving vengeance to the Lord.[30] We are not wishing a violent death on our ideological enemies. God forbid! Rather, we
long for their repentance and their salvation.

That being said, there's a key lesson to learn from the account.
Jehu, who had been anointed by a prophet on behalf of Elisha,
had just killed Jezebel's son Joram, and now he was about to
confront the woman herself. After she greeted him from a
window with both seduction and sarcasm, "he lifted up his
face toward the window and said, 'Who is on my side? Who?'
And two or three eunuchs looked down to him. He said, 'Drop
her down.' So they dropped her down and some of her blood
splattered on the wall and on the horses. Then he trampled
her" (2 Kings 9:32–33). And this is the most striking part of
the whole account: she who emasculated men was cast down
by emasculated men—literally emasculated, as in castrated.

Even castrated men can take a stand and regain their strength and virility. They did, and she was cast down.

In a spiritual sense this is starting to happen on college campuses in America, where men—yes, men!—are rising up to fight against pornography. They recognize that porn distorts their real manhood, not to mention debases women, and they are fighting back. As reported on The Daily Beast on December 6, 2018, "Republicans and radical feminists have all but abandoned it, but the fight against porn has an unlikely new champion: college men. Combining the energy of the #MeToo movement with a moral fervor, students at universities across the country told The Daily Beast they are working to get pornography off their campuses."[31] The effort was started by eighty Notre Dame University male students in October 2018. They "penned an open letter requesting a porn filter on the campus WiFi,"[32] and now students from other campuses, men and women alike, are saying, "Do it here too!"

Without a doubt Jezebel hates women and attacks them too. Without a doubt she has destroyed many a woman's life, including many a godly woman. And anytime there is a strong, anointed woman of God with a calling on her life, some insecure male leader is sure to brand *her* a Jezebel. How ironic and how ugly.

But allow me to focus for one final moment on the men of America, specifically the born-again, Bible-believing men. Many of you have been emasculated by sexual sin, stealing your confidence and your manhood, making you into a self-condemning slave. Others have been emasculated by the spirit of radical feminism, causing you to doubt yourself and shrink from a leadership role in your home. Others have been emasculated by spiritual intimidation, because of which you stay clear of conflict and confrontation. Still others have been emasculated by an apparent failure in faith, because of which you have become cautious and calculating, not wanting to be embarrassed or disappointed again.

My friends, you must not let Jezebel win! Our nation needs you. Our families need you. Our children need you. Our pulpits need you. As expressed by A. W. Tozer, "Yes, if evangelical Christianity is to stay alive she must have men again, the right kind of men. She must repudiate the weaklings who dare not speak out, and she must seek in prayer and much humility the coming again of men of the stuff prophets and martyrs are made of."[33]

My brothers, we need you to take hold of biblical manhood, using Jesus as your example (rather than some beer-guzzling TV tough guy). We need you to stand tall. To be strong. To lead well. To be spiritual. To mix compassion with toughness and humility with courage.

It doesn't matter what has spiritually or emotionally castrated you in the past, be it your upbringing or dynamics in your marriage or denominational politics or a moral failure. Jesus is a redeemer and a restorer, and with His help you can become a real man, a biblical man, a godly man.

Jezebel may have ruled you for many years, but it's time to cast her down. Get her out of your head, your heart, and your life. Together, as we stand by ones and twos, by tens and twenties, by hundreds and thousands, by millions and tens of millions, both men and women together, we will see this wicked stronghold defeated. Jezebel is coming down!

NOTES

CHAPTER 1: THE MOST WICKED WOMAN IN THE WORD OF GOD

1. Pray Alabama, "Pray Against Witchcraft Coming Against President Trump," Facebook, August 20, 2018, 5:27 p.m., https://www.facebook.com/116678935084921/videos/241848136380412/.

2. John Kilpatrick, "Containment," Church of His Presence, August 19, 2018, http://churchofhispresence.org/media/player/media/containment-2018/video/. See time stamp 2:01:50.

3. John Kilpatrick, "Containment," beginning at 2:02:07.

4. Greg Garrison, "Evangelical Christians See Trump As 'Man of God,'" *Jerusalem Post*, September 1, 2018, https://www.jpost.com/American-Politics/Evangelical-Christians-see-Trump-as-man-of-God-566249.

5. Jeroboam was the first king of the northern kingdom of Israel when it split from the southern kingdom of Judah. His principal sin was to make golden calves for the people to worship that were stationed in new temples he built in the north and south of his kingdom. (See 1 Kings 12:26–31.)

6. Urban Dictionary, s.v. "Jezebel," accessed April 6, 2019, https://www.urbandictionary.com/define.php?term=Jezebel.

7. In the words of Elijah, who called Ahab "he that troubles Israel" (1 Kings 18:17; see also vv. 16, 18).

8. See 1 Kings 21:20–29.

9. The NIV translates this as "urged on by Jezebel his wife." The NET Bible has "urged on by his wife Jezebel." The JPS Tanakh and Tree of Life Version have "at the instigation of his wife Jezebel."

10.   Tanna d'Bei Eliyahu Rabba 9, cited in Yishai Chasidah, *Encyclopedia of Biblical Personalities: Anthologized From the Talmud, Midrash and Rabbinic Writings* (New York: Mesorah Press, 1994), 81.

11.   Tanna d'Bei Eliyahu Rabba 10.

12.   Josephus, *Against Apion* 1.18, quoting the historian Menander, accessed April 2, 2019, http://www.gutenberg.org /files/2849/2849-h/2849-h.htm.

13.   Blue Letter Bible, s.v. *"Ethba'al,"* accessed April 6, 2019, https://www.blueletterbible.org/lang/lexicon/lexicon.cfm?Strongs =H856&t=KJV.

14.   G. A. Yee, "Jezebel (Person)," in David Noel Freedman, ed., *The Anchor Yale Bible Dictionary*, vol. 3 (New York: Doubleday, 1992), 848–849 with reference to Althayah Brenner-Idan, *The Israelite Woman* (Sheffield, England: Sheffield, 1985).

15.   Yee, "Jezebel."

16.   Another way of translating this verse is "I will reserve seven thousand in Israel who have not bowed their knees to Baal."

17.   To explain how Elijah could have seen God move so miraculously on Mount Carmel yet fear for his life just a few verses later, nineteenth-century preacher Charles Spurgeon offered this theory: "The message from Jezebel, that he would be slain the next morning, was probably not so terrible to him as the discovery that came with it that his great demonstration against Baal was doomed to be a failure. The proud Sidonian queen would still rule over vacillating Ahab and, through Ahab, she would still keep power over the people—and the idol gods would sit safely on their thrones. The thought was gall and wormwood to the idol-hating Prophet. He became so despondent that he was ready to give up the conflict and to quit the battlefield. He could not bear to live in the land where the people were so blindly infatuated as to honor Baal and to dishonor Jehovah. He resolved to leave right away." See C. H. Spurgeon, "The Still Small Voice" (sermon, Metropolitan Tabernacle, London, July 9, 1892), https://www.ccel.org/ccel/spurgeon /sermons28.xxxii.html.

18.   Joseph Parker, *These Sayings of Mine: Pulpit Notes on Seven Chapters of the First Gospel, and Other Sermons* (London:

Forgotten Books, 2017), 62, https://www.amazon.com/These
-Sayings-Mine-Chapters-Sermons/dp/1332916929.

19. See 1 Kings 21:23 with 2 Kings 9:10, 30–37.

20. Scott Morefield, "Watch: Protesters Try to Claw Supreme
Court Doors Open During Kavanaugh's Swearing In," The Daily
Caller, October 7, 2018, https://dailycaller.com/2018/10/07
/protesters-claw-supreme-court-doors/.

CHAPTER 2: JEZEBEL IS ALIVE AND WELL IN AMERICA TODAY

1. For books about the Jezebel spirit see Bill Vincent,
*Destroying the Jezebel Spirit: How to Overcome the Spirit Before
It Destroys You!* (Litchfield, IL: Revival Waves of Glory Books &
Publishing, 2014); John Paul Jackson, *Unmasking the Jezebel Spirit*
(Flower Mound, TX: Streams Books, 2002); and Steve Sampson,
Confronting Jezebel: Discerning and Defeating the Spirit of Control
(Grand Rapids, MI: Chosen Books, 2012).

2. "Jezebel, the 'Mainstream' of Feminism," Media Research
Center, accessed April 6, 2019, https://www.mrc.org/bozells
-column/jezebel-mainstream-feminism. Obviously, Jezebel is first
and foremost a reference to the Old Testament queen.

3. Jezebel (@Jezebel), "Gender, culture, and politics. With
teeth. Delivered straight to your inbox ~ TRA TRA," Twitter,
November 15, 2018, 8:42 p.m., https://twitter.com/jezebel/status
/1063291292581593088.

4. "Jezebel, the 'Mainstream' of Feminism," Media Research
Center.

5. Anna Holmes, ed., *The Book of Jezebel: An Illustrated
Encyclopedia of Lady Things* (New York: Grand Central Publishing,
2013). Under the entry on "Jezebel," the book explains that "by
2007, [Jezebel] was snappy shorthand for a woman of ill repute,
which made it the perfect name for Gawker Media's new ladyblog."

6. "Jezebel, the 'Mainstream' of Feminism," Media Research
Center.

7. Holmes, *The Book of Jezebel*, loc. 5343–5346, Kindle.

8. Encyclopedia.com, s.v. "Baal (Semitic, Ba'al; 'Master, Lord'),"
accessed April 6, 2019, https://www.encyclopedia.com/politics

/dictionaries-thesauruses-pictures-and-press-releases/baal-semitic
-baal-master-lord.

9.   New World Encyclopedia, s.v. "El," accessed April 6, 2019, http://www.newworldencyclopedia.org/entry/El.

10.   Ray Vander Laan, "Fertility Cults of Canaan," Focus on the Family, accessed April 6, 2019, https://www.thattheworldmayknow .com/fertility-cults-of-canaan.

11.   Vander Laan, "Fertility Cults of Canaan."

12.   Vander Laan, "Fertility Cults of Canaan."

13.   See Karin Finsterbusch, Armin Lange, and K. F. Diethard Römheld, eds., *Human Sacrifice in Jewish and Christian Tradition* (Leiden, Netherlands: E. J. Brill, 2007), 112. For the most recent relevant study see Heath D. Dewrell, *Child Sacrifice in Ancient Israel* (Winona Lake, IN: Eisenbrauns, 2017).

14.   Eugene H. Merrill, *Deuteronomy* (Nashville: Broadman & Holman Publishers, 1994), 228.

15.   See, for example, the New International Version, Tree of Life Version, and New Living Translation. A related word is found in Exodus 22:18, rendered this way in the King James Version: "Thou shalt not suffer a witch to live." Virtually all modern translations use "sorceress" rather than "witch," but it's clear the concepts are closely related.

16.   Benjamin Fearnow, "Number of Witches Rises Dramatically Across U.S. as Millennials Reject Christianity," *Newsweek*, November 18, 2018, https://www.newsweek.com/witchcraft -wiccans-mysticism-astrology-witches-millennials-pagans -religion-1221019.

17.   See Himaja Merugumuvvala, "Kanakadurga Temple, Vijayawada," *Hey Krishna* (blog), October 19, 2012, http:// blogheykrishna.blogspot.com/2012/10/kanakadurga-temple vijayawada.html, for some mythological details, as well as for the image I described.

18.   See Michael L. Brown, *Revolution! The Call to Holy War* (Ventura, CA: Regal Books, 2000); idem, *Revolution in the Church: Challenging the Religious System With a Call to Radical Change* (Grand Rapids, MI: Chosen, 2002).

CHAPTER 3: JEZEBEL AND IDOLATRY

1.   For Terah as an idolater, see Joshua 24:2.

2.   "Bereishit [Genesis] Rabbah 38," Sefaria, accessed April 6, 2019, https://www.sefaria.org/Bereishit_Rabbah.38.13?lang=en&wit h=all&lang2=en. For this same tradition in the Quran, see the first link in this note, as well as "The Story of Abraham and Idols in the Qur'an and Midrash Genesis Rabbah," Islamic Awareness, updated January 8, 2006, https://www.islamic-awareness.org/quran/sources /bbrabbah.

3.   Pandit Dasa, "The 33 Million Gods of Hinduism," Huff-Post, updated October 6, 2012, https://www.huffingtonpost.com /gadadhara-pandit-dasa/the-33-million-demigods-o_b_1737207 .html.

4.   Sreelekha Radhamma, "Time to Stop This Yearly Crime in the Name of Faith!," *Sreelekha IPS* (blog), February 27, 2018, http:// sreelekhaips.blogspot.com/2018/02/time-to-stop-this-yearly-crime -in-name.html. I do not believe this was connected with the march I observed. For a related story see Melody Zaccheus, "Live Music at Thaipusam After 42 years," *Straits Times*, January 18, 2016, https:// www.straitstimes.com/singapore/live-music-at-thaipusam -after-42-years.

5.   For our documentary on his amazing conversion, *From Son of Sam to Son of Hope*, see https://askdrbrown.myshopify.com /products/son-of-sam-son-of-hope-dvd.

6.   Scott Bonn, "Serial Killer David Berkowitz, aka Son of Sam, Tells Professor 'I Was Once an Evil Person' in Prison Conversation," CBS News, updated August 7, 2017, https://www.cbsnews.com /news/serial-killer-david-berkowitz-aka-son-of-sam-tells-professor -i-was-once-an-evil-person-in-prison-conversation/.

7.   Bonn, "Serial Killer David Berkowitz."

8.   Bonn, "Serial Killer David Berkowitz," emphasis added.

9.   A. W. Tozer, "The Old Cross and the New," *Alliance Weekly* 81, no. 41 (October 12, 1946), 645, https://www.cmalliance.org /resources/archives/alifepdf/AW-1946-10-12.pdf.

10.   A. W. Tozer, *The Knowledge of the Holy* (New York: Harper-Collins, 1961), 3, https://books.google.com/books?id=7qMko7zf cqIC&q.

11.   Tozer, *The Knowledge of the Holy*, 3–4.

12.   Tozer, *The Knowledge of the Holy*, 4.

13.   See "Rashi on Exodus 32:6:2," Sefaria, accessed April 6, 2019, https://www.sefaria.org/Rashi_on_Exodus.32.6.2?lang=en. He provides textual support for his argument.

14.   These paragraphs were quoted from Brown, *Revolution!*,105. It is based on a firsthand account from my late friend Art Katz, the man who asked Pastor Wurmbrand the question related in this story.

CHAPTER 4: JEZEBEL AND THE SEXUAL SEDUCTION OF AMERICA

1.   "20 Mind-Blowing Stats About the Porn Industry and Its Underage Consumers," Fight the New Drug, January 3, 2019, https://fightthenewdrug.org/10-porn-stats-that-will-blow-your -mind/.

2.   "Most Popular Retail Websites in the United States as of December 2017, Ranked by Visitors (in Millions)," Statista, accessed April 6, 2019, https://www.statista.com/statistics/271450/monthly -unique-visitors-to-us-retail-websites/.

3.   Laila Mickelwait, "A Reflection on the Casualties of Playboy," Exodus Cry, October 29, 2015, https://exoduscry.com /blog/general/a-reflection-on-the-casualties-of-playboy/, emphasis in the original.

4.   "Consider This," Novus Project, accessed April 6, 2019, http://thenovusproject.org/resource-hub/parents, emphasis added.

5.   Kristin MacLaughlin, "The Detrimental Effects of Pornography on Small Children," Net Nanny, December 19, 2017, https:// www.netnanny.com/blog/the-detrimental-effects-of-pornography -on-small-children/.

6.   Monica Gabriel Marshall, "Divorce Lawyers Say This Is Why Marriages Are Falling Apart," Verily, July 28, 2017, https:// verilymag.com/2017/07/causes-of-divorce-effects-of-watching -pornography.

7.   George A. Akerlof and Janet L. Yellen, "An Analysis of Out-of-Wedlock Births in the United States," Brookings Institution, August 1, 1996, https://www.brookings.edu/research/an-analysis-of -out-of-wedlock-births-in-the-united-states/.

8.   Lindsay M. Monte and Renee R. Ellis, "Fertility of Women in the United States: 2012," US Census Bureau, July 2014, https:// www.census.gov/content/dam/Census/library/publications/2014 /demo/p20-575.pdf.

9.   Office of Adolescent Health, "Adolescent Development and STDs," US Department of Health & Human Services, last reviewed March 28, 2019, https://www.hhs.gov/ash/oah/adolescent -development/reproductive-health-and-teen-pregnancy/stds /index.html.

10.   Richard Morgan, "Ashley Madison Is Back—and Claims Surprising User Numbers," *New York Post*, May 21, 2017, https:// nypost.com/2017/05/21/ashley-madison-is-back-and-claims -surprising-user-numbers/.

11.   Tim Baysinger, "No More 'Taxicab Confessions': HBO Removes All of Its Adult Entertainment Programming," TheWrap, August 28, 2018, https://www.thewrap.com/hbo-quietly-removed -all-of-its-adult-entertainment/.

12.   Mellissa Withers, "Pimp Culture Glorification and Sex Trafficking," *Psychology Today*, April 28, 2017, https://www .psychologytoday.com/us/blog/modern-day-slavery/201704/pimp -culture-glorification-and-sex-trafficking.

13.   David Finkelhor, Richard Ormrod, and Mark Chaffin, "Juveniles Who Commit Sex Offenses Against Minors," *Juvenile Justice Bulletin* (December 2009), 3, http://unh.edu/ccrc/pdf/CV171 .pdf.

14.   John Stonestreet and Anne Morse, "The Sexual Revolution's Latest Victims: Children Abusing Children," *Christian Post*, January 4, 2019, https://www.christianpost.com/voice/the-sexual -revolutions-latest-victims-children-abusing-children.html.

15.   International Labour Organization and Walk Free Foundation, *Global Estimates of Modern Slavery* (Geneva: ILO Publications, 2017), 11; https://www.ilo.org/wcmsp5/groups/public /---dgreports/---dcomm/documents/publication/wcms_575479.pdf.

16. "Human Trafficking Statistics: The Meaning," *ERASE Child Trafficking* (blog), July 20, 2016, https://www.erasechildtrafficking .org/statistics-of-human-trafficking/, emphasis in the original.

17. "Key Facts," National Center for Missing & Exploited Children, accessed April 6, 2019, http://www.missingkids.com/footer /media/keyfacts#exploitedchildrenstatistics; Melissa Stroebel and Stacy Jeleniewski, *Global Research Project* (New York: National Center for Missing & Exploited Children, 2015), http://www .missingkids.com/content/dam/pdfs/ncmec-analysis/grp.pdf.

18. Mary L. Pulido, "Child Pornography: Basic Facts About a Horrific Crime," HuffPost, updated January 23, 2014, https://www .huffingtonpost.com/mary-l-pulido-phd/child-pornography-basic -f_b_4094430.html.

19. Michael Brown, "The Death of Hugh Hefner and the End of the Sexual Revolution," *Christian Post,* September 28, 2017, https://www.christianpost.com/news/the-death-of-hugh-hefner -and-the-end-of-the-sexual-revolution-200895/.

20. Gary Wilson, *Your Brain on Porn: Internet Pornography and the Emerging Science of Addiction*, rev. ed. (n.p.: Commonwealth Publishing, 2017), loc. 113–115, Kindle.

21. Wilson, *Your Brain on Porn*, loc. 150–159.

22. See Michael L. Brown, *Saving a Sick America* (Nashville: Thomas Nelson, 2017), 127–128.

23. Babylonian Talmud, Sanhedrin 39b, accessed April 6, 2019, https://juchre.org/talmud/sanhedrin/sanhedrin2.htm#39b.

24. Wilson, *Your Brain on Porn.*

25. Wilson, *Your Brain on Porn*, loc. 88–92.

26. Luke Gilkerson, "Get the Latest Pornography Statistics," Covenant Eyes, February 19, 2013, http://www.covenanteyes .com/2013/02/19/pornography-statistics/.

CHAPTER 5: JEZEBEL AND THE SPIRIT OF BABY KILLING

1. Matthew Hoffman, "Famous Pro-Abortion Feminist Calls Unborn Child a 'Tumor,'" LifeSiteNews.com, November 23, 2010, https://www.lifesitenews.com/news/famous-pro-abortion-feminist -calls-unborn-child-a-tumor.

2.   Rashi's commentary to Jeremiah 7:31, as quoted in John Gill, "Commentary of Jeremiah 7:31," *The New John Gill Exposition of the Entire Bible*, accessed April 6, 2019, https://www.studylight. org/commentaries/geb/jeremiah-7.html. Rashi was a famous rabbi who lived from 1040–1105.

3.   Found in the compilation called Yalkut Shimoni (Yalkut of Rabbi Simeon), cited in Moses Margoliouth, *A Pilgrimage to the Land of My Fathers* (n.p.: Elibron Classics, 2007), 125, https://www .amazon.com/Pilgrimage-Land-My-Fathers/dp/0543674908.

4.   Cleitarchus, *Scholia* to Plato's *Republica* 337A, cited in Carrie Ann Murray, ed., *Diversity of Sacrifice: Form and Function of Sacrificial Practices in the Ancient World and Beyond* (Albany, NY: State University of New York Press, 2016), 106, https://books. google.com/books?id=IB0iDAAAQBAJ&pg. For a depiction of this practice from the 1914 silent movie *Cabiria* see PrayForGermantown, "Cabiria Video of Child Sacrifice," YouTube, June 11, 2014, https://www.youtube.com/watch?time_continue=79&v=QeqZ T6OcjJ0.

5.   Diodorus Siculus, *Library of History* 20.14.6, accessed April 6, 2019, http://penelope.uchicago.edu/Thayer/E/Roman/Texts /Diodorus_Siculus/20A*.html#3.

6.   John Milton, *Paradise Lost*, bk. 1, lines 392–396, https:// www.dartmouth.edu/~milton/reading_room/pl/book_1/text.shtml.

7.   Rachel Cox, "Abortion Methods: The Gruesome Reality of How Babies Are Killed in Abortion," LifeNews.com, February 17, 2014, https://www.lifenews.com/2014/02/17/abortion-methods-the -gruesome-reality-of-how-babies-are-killed-in-abortion/.

8.   Cox, "Abortion Methods."

9.   Cox, "Abortion Methods."

10.   National Right to Life Committee, Inc., *The State of Abortion in the United States* (Washington, DC: NRLC Communications, 2019), https://www.nrlc.org/uploads/communications /stateofabortion2019.pdf.

11.   Jerry Newcombe, "Abortion—Modern Child Sacrifice?," ChristianHeadlines.com, March 7, 2018, https://www .christianheadlines.com/columnists/guest-commentary/abortion -modern-child-sacrifice.html.

12. See Michael Brown, "New York Reveals Its Blood Lust for Baby Killing," AskDrBrown, January 25, 2019, https://askdrbrown .org/library/new-york-reveals-its-blood-lust-baby-killing.

13. Jonathon van Maren, "Here's What a Late-Term Abortion Is Really Like," LifeSiteNews.com, May 8, 2018, https://www.life sitenews.com/pulse/heres-what-a-late-term-abortion-is-really-like.

14. "Testimony of Brenda Pratt Shafer, R.N., Subcommittee on the Constitution," March 21, 1996, House Judiciary Committee Homepage, https://web.archive.org/web/19970430081149/https:// www.house.gov/judiciary/215.htm.

15. "Testimony of Brenda Pratt Shafer."

16. NBC News, "Michelle Wolf's Uncensored White House Correspondents' Dinner Speech (Full)," YouTube, April 28, 2018, https://www.youtube.com/watch?v=6HTggNxOGWw.

17. Victoria Woodhull and Tennessee Claflin, "The Slaughter of the Innocents," *Woodhull and Claflin's Weekly*, June 20, 1874, 8.

18. Susan B. Anthony, "Marriage and Maternity," *The Revolution*, July 8, 1969, 4, https://susanbanthonyhouse.org/blog/the -revolution-july-8-1869/.

19. Sarah F. Norton, "Tragedy—Social and Domestic," *Woodhull and Claflin's Weekly*, November 19, 1870, 11.

20. Elizabeth Cady Stanton, "Infanticide and Prostitution," *The Revolution*, February 5, 1868, 65, https://archive.org/details /revolution-1868-02-05/page/n1.

21. Lorenzo Jensen III, "The 25 All-Time Greatest Pro-Choice Quotes," Thought Catalog, July 16, 2015, https://thoughtcatalog .com/lorenzo-jensen-iii/2015/07/the-25-all-time-greatest-pro .choice-quotes/.

22. Amelia Bonow and Emily Nokes, eds., *Shout Your Abortion* (Oakland, CA: PM Press, 2018), foreword, https://books.google .com/books?id=MVFtDwAAQBAJ&pg.

23. HiHo Kids, "Kids Meet Someone Who's Had an Abortion," YouTube, December 18, 2018, https://www.youtube.com/watch ?v=ZXKclYbp8gA. Please note that this video was removed. It has been reported that Shout Your Abortion will be releasing a book just for children. See Amelia Bonow, "I let a bunch of kids grill

me about my abortion and it was great. #ShoutYourAbortion will be releasing a children's book about abortion in 2020!," Twitter, December 28, 2018, 5:29 p.m., https://twitter.com/ameliabonow /status/1078825207203356672.

24. HiHo Kids, "Kids Meet Someone Who's Had an Abortion."

25. Bonow and Nokes, *Shout Your Abortion*, foreword.

26. Bonow and Nokes, *Shout Your Abortion*, preface.

27. See Michael Brown, "The Governor of Virginia: Let's Be Civil About Killing Newborns," AskDrBrown, February 2, 2019, https://askdrbrown.org/library/governor-virginia-let%E2%80%99s- be-civil-about-killing-newborns. More broadly, see Georgi Boorman, "Infanticide Is the Historical Hallmark of a Pagan Culture," *The Federalist*, February 4, 2019, http://thefederalist. com/2019/02/04/without-christianity-we-might-unthinkingly- return-to-the-infanticidal-cultures-of-yore/#.XFhWYJbTMFQ. twitter; and Wesley J. Smith, "Infanticide Becomes Justifiable," *First Things*, February 6, 2019, https://www.firstthings.com/web -exclusives/2019/02/infanticide-becomes-justifiable.

28. For example, go to AskDrBrown, "Turning Hearts and Changing Minds to Pro-Life," YouTube, November 13, 2018, https://www.youtube.com/watch?v=-QZ4-vXWqSA, and Ask- DrBrown, "Two Tearful Calls on Abortion," YouTube, July 20, 2015, https://www.youtube.com/watch?v=nqfzJdYXxKg.

29. AskDrBrown, "Christian Working at Planned Parenthood Vows Never to Return: 'It's Not Tissue! They Are Babies!'" YouTube, July 29, 2017, https://www.youtube.com/watch?v=BSmnPhAWU0c.

30. Kelli, "Former Planned Parenthood Manager Speaks: We Placed Grief Journals in the Recovery Room," Live Action, December 26, 2017, https://www.liveaction.org/news/planned -parenthood-manager-grief-journals/.

31. Kelli, "Former Planned Parenthood Manager Speaks."

32. AskDrBrown, "Christian Working at Planned Parenthood Vows Never to Return," https://www.youtube.com/watch?v=BSm nPhAWU0c&feature=youtu.be&t=359. The video at this link is queued up to start where Crystal talks about the POC room.

33. Bonow and Nokes, *Shout Your Abortion*, El Sanchez.

34.   See, for example, Rebecca Traister, "Abortion/reproductive justice are not 'cultural' issues; they are not 'social' issues. This is about economic equality and public health," Twitter, April 22, 2017, 9:53 a.m., https://twitter.com/rtraister/status/855826950111277061.

35.   Michael Brown, "Prepare for the Wrath of the Pro-Abortion Militants," The Stream, September 20, 2018, https://stream.org/prepare-wrath-pro-abortion-militants/.

36.   Jennifer Hartline, "It's Not Kavanaugh. It's Roe," The Stream, September 20, 2018, https://stream.org/not-kavanaugh-roe/.

37.   Hartline, "It's Not Kavanaugh."

38.   Hartline, "It's Not Kavanaugh."

39.   Hartline, "It's Not Kavanaugh," emphasis in the original.

40.   As quoted in Sam Morris, "Open by the Permission of the Church?," *Samuel A. Morris* (blog), August 26, 2015, http://samuel amorris.blogspot.com/2015/08/open-by-permission-of-church.html.

41.   Francis A. Schaeffer, *A Christian Manifesto* (Wheaton, IL: Crossway Books, 1981), 73–74, https://www.amazon.com/Christian -Manifesto-Francis-Schaeffer/dp/1581346921.

42.   Although marches for life and large-scale rallies get a lot of attention, the vast majority of Christians do very little when it comes to fighting abortion.

43.   See US House of Representatives Select Investigative Panel of the Energy & Commerce Committee, "Final Report," December 30, 2016, https://archives-energycommerce.house.gov/sites /republicans.energycommerce.house.gov/files/documents/Select _Investigative_Panel_Final_Report.pdf; and Orange County District Attorney, "OCDA Obtains $7.8 Million Settlement and Admission of Liability in Lawsuit Against Two Companies Who Unlawfully Sold Fetal Tissue and Cells for Profit," Orange County District Attorney News Release, December 8, 2017, https://web.archive.org /web/20180925003102/http://orangecountyda.org/civica/press /display.asp?layout=2&Entry=5406.

44.   Statistic reported by Worldometers, quoted in Thomas D. Williams, "Abortion Leading Cause of Death in 2018 With 41 Million Killed," Breitbart, December 31, 2018, https://www.breitbart .com/health/2018/12/31/abortion-leading-cause-of-death-in-2018 -with-41-million-killed/.

CHAPTER 6: JEZEBEL AND RADICAL FEMINISM

1.   Rebecca Traister, *Good and Mad: The Revolutionary Power of Women's Anger* (New York: Simon & Schuster, 2018).

2.   Alice Walker, "To Be a Woman," as quoted in Traister, *Good and Mad*, vii.

3.   Traister, *Good and Mad*, xvi.

4.   Traister, *Good and Mad*, xx.

5.   To be honest, even in a satirical, feminist compilation like *The Book of Jezebel* (see chapter 2), the authors make plenty of points with which I agree. Real misogyny (rather than the imagined kind) is always wrong.

6.   See Jory Micah, "The Rise of Evangelical Feminism," *Relevant*, March 29, 2016, https://relevantmagazine.com/god/god-our-generation/rise-evangelical-feminism. For a critical assessment see Wayne Grudem, *Evangelical Feminism: A New Path to Liberalism?* (Wheaton, IL: Crossway, 2006). According to *The Book of Jezebel*, *feminist* is defined as "person who believes in the political, economic, and social equality of the sexes. Period" (Holmes, 100).

7.   E.g., Luke 8:1–2; Mark 16:1–7; Romans 16:1–15.

8.   Emma Kate Fittes, James Briggs, and Domenica Bongiovanni, "IU Health Says Nurse 'No Longer An Employee' Following Controversial Tweet," *Indy Star*, November 26, 2017, https://www.indystar.com/story/news/local/2017/11/26/iu-health-says-nurse-no-longer-employee-following-controversial-tweet/896178001/. For the record, the tweet was so extreme that it cost Baker her job.

9.   Emily Lindin (@EmilyLindin), "Here's an unpopular opinion: I'm actually not at all concerned about innocent men losing their jobs over false sexual assault/harassment allegations," Twitter, November 21, 2017, 12:45 p.m., https://twitter.com/EmilyLindin/status/933073784822579200.

10.   Emily Lindin (@EmilyLindin), "Sorry. If some innocent men's reputations have to take a hit in the process of undoing the patriarchy, that is a price I am absolutely willing to pay," Twitter, November 21, 2017, 12:49 p.m., https://twitter.com/EmilyLindin/status/933074980627030016.

11.   See Jone Johnson Lewis, "What Is Radical Feminism?" ThoughtCo, updated August 9, 2018, https://www.thoughtco.com /what-is-radical-feminism-3528997.

12.   Jake Fillis, "23 Quotes From Feminists That Will Make You Rethink Feminism," Thought Catalog, May 17, 2014, https:// thoughtcatalog.com/jake-fillis/2014/05/23-quotes-from-feminists -that-will-make-you-rethink-feminism/.

13.   Ariel Levy, "Goodbye Again," *New Yorker*, April 14, 2008, https://www.newyorker.com/magazine/2008/04/21/goodbye-again.

14.   "Home," Linda Gordon, accessed April 6, 2019, http://www .lindagordonhistorian.org/.

15.   Ariel Levy, "The Prisoner of Sex," *New York*, accessed April 6, 2019, http://nymag.com/nymetro/news/people/features/11907/.

16.   Sheila Cronan, "Marriage," *Radical Feminism*, Anne Koedt, Ellen Levine, and Anita Rapone, eds. (Chicago: Quadrangle Books, 1973), http://feminist-reprise.org/docs/RF/MARRIAGE.pdf. (Her name is sometimes misspelled as Cronin.)

17.   "Honoring Diversity and Courage," *Oregon Outlook* (Summer 2009), 5, https://cpb-us-e1.wpmucdn.com/blogs.uoregon. edu/dist/a/1278/files/2013/02/Summer-2009-Outlook-Honoring -Diversity-and-Courage-osdn92.pdf.

18.   "Mary Daly," Liberation Theologies Online Library, accessed January 30, 2019, https://liberationtheology.org/people -organizations/mary-daly/.

19.   Germaine Greer, *The Female Eunuch* (New York: Harper-Collins, 2009).

20.   Leon Trotsky, *Women and the Family* (New York: Pathfinder Press, 2011), 54, https://www.amazon.com/Women-Family -Leon-Trotsky/dp/0873482182. See also Ana Muñoz and Alan Woods, "Marxism and the Emancipation of Women," In Defence of Marxism, March 8, 2000, https://www.marxist.com/marxism -feminism-emancipation-women080300.htm. See further K. Z. Howell, *Broken: The Rise of Radical Feminism and the Decline of Western Civilization* (n.p.: n.p., 2017).

21.   Joreen, in *Radical Feminism*, 52.

22.   See Robert Jensen, *The End of Patriarchy: Radical Feminism for Men* (North Melbourne, Victoria, Australia: Spinifex Press, 2017).

23.   Fox News, "The Duke Men's Project, launched this month and hosted by the campus Women's Center, offers a nine-week program...," Facebook, October 1, 2016, https://www.facebook.com /FoxNews/posts/10154658931601336. Note also that only male-identified individuals can attend, which presumably means that: 1) a man who identifies as a woman cannot attend; and 2) a woman who identifies as a man can attend, in which case, how is a male-identified female connected to toxic masculinity? (If I'm missing something here, be assured that I'm trying my best to report this accurately and not simply being sarcastic.)

24.   Editorial Board, "Engendering Gender Harmony," *The Chronicle*, September 29, 2016, https://web.archive.org /web/20160930174102/http://www.dukechronicle.com/article /2016/09/engendering-gender-harmony.

25.   Editorial Board, "Engendering Gender Harmony."

26.   Jillian Kay Melchior, "Duke Offers Men a 'Safe Space' to Contemplate Their 'Toxic Masculinity,'" Heat Street, September 30, 2016, https://web.archive.org/web/20161002110556/http://heatst .com/culture-wars/duke-offers-men-a-safe-space-to-contemplate -their-toxic-masculinity/.

27.   "A Rogue's Gallery of Wretched Misogynists," in Holmes, *The Book of Jezebel*, 184–185.

28.   Allen West's speech for Women Impacting the Nation, April 19, 2011, Boca Raton, Florida, available at AmericanPatriotsPres, "ALLEN WEST W.I.N. MEETING PART 2," YouTube, April 21, 2011, https://www.youtube.com/watch?v=Px4f4vTpXg0. For a critical assessment see Tanya Somanader, "Allen West: Liberal Women Are 'Neutering American Men,'" ThinkProgress, April 25, 2011, https://thinkprogress.org/allen-west-liberal-women-are -neutering-american-men-f82635486505/, which refers to West's "blatant misogyny."

29.   Irin Carmon, "Delusional Congressman Says Planned Parenthood Is 'Neutering' Men," Jezebel, April 25, 2011, https://

jezebel.com/delusional-congressman-says-planned-parenthood-is-neut-30818198.

30. For the trauma this can cause, see Anonymous Us, https://anonymousus.org/.

31. John Tierney, "The Doofus Dad," *New York Times*, June 18, 2005, https://www.nytimes.com/2005/06/18/opinion/the-doofus-dad.html.

32. Tierney, "The Doofus Dad."

33. Sarah Petersen, "Dumbing Down Dad: How Media Present Husbands, Fathers as Useless," *Deseret News*, February 27, 2013, https://www.deseretnews.com/article/865574236/Dumbing-down-Dad-How-media-present-husbands-fathers-as-useless.html.

34. Courtney Kane, "Men Are Becoming the Ad Target of the Gender Sneer," *New York Times*, January 28, 2005, https://www.nytimes.com/2005/01/28/business/media/men-are-becoming-the-ad-target-of-the-gender-sneer.html.

35. Melissa Steward, "How Mass Media Portray Dads & What You Can Do About It," *The Father Factor* (blog), National Fatherhood Initiative, July 2, 2015, https://www.fatherhood.org/fatherhood/americas-fatherhood-problem-mass-media-and-how-we-can-fix-it, emphasis in the original.

36. John Adams, "Representation of Men, Masculinity and Fathers in the Media," *UK Dad Blog: Fatherhood, Parenting, Family and Lifestyle* (blog), November 27, 2017, https://dadbloguk.com/representation-men-masculinity-fathers-media/.

37. Tom Ciccotta, "Princeton Wants Students to Stop Using the Word 'Man,'" Breitbart, August 18, 2016, https://www.breitbart.com/tech/2016/08/18/princeton-wants-students-stop-using-word-man/.

38. "Guidelines for Using Gender Inclusive Language," Princeton University, March 2015, https://web.archive.org/web/20160818124949/https://www.princeton.edu/hr/progserv/communications/inclusivelanguage.pdf.

39. "Guidelines for Using Gender Inclusive Language," Princeton University.

40.   "Guidelines for Using Gender Inclusive Language," Princeton University. For my sarcastic response to this see Michael L. Brown, "Response to Princeton U Banning the 'M' Word," AskDrBrown, August 21, 2016, https://askdrbrown.org/library /response-princeton-u-banning-%E2%80%98m%E2%80%99-word; for my video response see Michael L. Brown, "Princeton University STOP Using the M Word," AskDrBrown, August 21, 2016, https:// askdrbrown.org/library/princeton-university-stop-using-m-word.

41.   "Feminist Declares the Invention of the Alphabet the Root of Sexism, Misogyny and Patriarchy," Weasel Zippers, August 5, 2016, https://www.weaselzippers.us/287910-feminist-declares-the -invention-of-the-alphabet-the-root-of-sexism-misogyny-and -patriarchy/; Maria Popova, "How the Invention of the Alphabet Usurped Female Power in Society and Sparked the Rise of Patriarchy in Human Culture," Brain Pickings, March 17, 2014, https:// www.brainpickings.org/2014/03/17/shlain-alphabet-goddess/.

42.   Popova, "How the Invention of the Alphabet Usurped Female Power in Society and Sparked the Rise of Patriarchy in Human Culture." According to the online biography at Amazon, Shlain is the "chief of laparoscopic surgery at California Medical Center in San Francisco" (see "The Alphabet Versus the Goddess: The Conflict Between Word and Image," Amazon, accessed January 31, 2019, https://www.amazon.com/Alphabet-Versus-Goddess -Conflict-Between/dp/0140196013).

43.   "Survey: Some Say Santa Should Be Rebranded Female, Gender Neutral," ABC Inc., KGO-TV San Francisco, December 14, 2018, https://abc7news.com/society/should-santa-be-rebranded -female-gender-neutral/4899604/.

44.   "Survey," ABC Inc., KGO-TV San Francisco.

45.   Calvin Freiburger, "Survey Claims 27% Want Female or 'Gender-Neutral' Santa, Despite Roots as Historical Figure," LifeSite News.com, December 17, 2018, https://www.lifesitenews.com/news /survey-claims-27-want-female-or-gender-neutral-santa-despite -roots-as-histo.

46.   Nathan Wold, "10 of the Craziest Ideas Pushed in the Name of Feminism," Listverse, December 25, 2014, http://listverse.

com/2014/12/25/10-of-the-craziest-ideas-pushed-in-the-name-of
-feminism/.

47.   Wold, "10 of the Craziest Ideas Pushed in the Name of Feminism."

48.   Wikipedia, s.v. "Luce Irigaray," last edited January 24, 2019, 06:37, https://en.wikipedia.org/wiki/Luce_Irigaray.

49.   Wold, "10 of the Craziest Ideas Pushed in the Name of Feminism."

50.   Esther Rabbah 3:2, cited in Chasidah, *Encyclopedia of Biblical Personalities*, 81.

51.   Rodney Stark, *The Rise of Christianity: How the Obscure, Marginal Jesus Movement Became the Dominant Religious Force in the Western World in a Few Centuries* (Princeton, NJ: Princeton Univ. Press, 1996).

52.   Mark Tapson, "Houston Rescuers Prove the Lie of 'Toxic Masculinity,'" Acculturated, August 31, 2017, https://acculturated.com/houston-rescuers-prove-lie-toxic-masculinity/.

53.   Tapson, "Houston Rescuers Prove the Lie of 'Toxic Masculinity.'"

54.   The two occupations with the highest fatal work injury rates include 1) fishers and fishing-related workers and 2) logging workers. While the Bureau of Labor Statistics (BLS) does not have gender data specifically for fishers and fishing related workers, 75.7 percent of those in farming, fishing, and forestry occupations are male. BLS data indicates 97.4 percent of logging workers are male. In the other occupations with the highest fatal work-injury rates the percentage of males ranges from 74.2 percent to 97.8 percent. These numbers for the most dangerous jobs cannot simply be explained based on cultural habit. Overall, for all workers of all occupations, 53.1 percent are male. See Bureau of Labor Statistics, "National Census of Fatal Occupational Injuries in 2017," news release, December 18, 2018, https://www.bls.gov/news.release/pdf/cfoi.pdf, chart 3; and "Labor Force Statistics From the Current Population Survey," Bureau of Labor Statistics, last modified January 18, 2019, https://www.bls.gov/cps/cpsaat11.htm.

55.   See Acts 18:2, 18, 26; Romans 16:3; 1 Corinthians 16:19; 2 Timothy 4:19. (Priscilla is sometimes called Prisca.)

56. As rendered in the New American Standard Bible, "Greet Andronicus and Junias, my kinsmen and my fellow prisoners, who are outstanding among the apostles, who also were in Christ before me" (Rom. 16:7); see also the NIV. Contrast the English Standard Version and Christian Standard Bible, which only see Junia as "well known to the apostles" or "noteworthy in the eyes of the apostles."

57. For example, see Mimi Haddad, "Egalitarian Pioneers: Betty Friedan or Catherine Booth?," *Priscilla Papers* 20, no. 4 (October 31, 2006), https://www.cbeinternational.org/resources /article/priscilla-papers/egalitarian-pioneers.

58. For a strong defense of the complementarian position (which I argue for, although with more flexibility than authors cited here) see Andreas J. Köstenberger and Thomas R. Schreiner, *Women in the Church: An Interpretation and Application of 1 Timothy 2:9–15*, 3rd ed. (Wheaton, IL: Crossway, 2016). For a strong defense of the egalitarian position, meaning there is complete ministry equality for males and females in the church, see Philip Barton Payne, *Man and Woman, One in Christ: An Exegetical and Theological Study of Paul's Letters* (Grand Rapids, MI: Zondervan, 2009). See also J. Lee Grady, *Ten Lies the Church Tells Women: How the Bible Has Been Misused to Keep Women in Spiritual Bondage*, rev. ed. (Lake Mary, FL: Charisma House, 2006). For other related studies see Ronald W. Pierce and Rebecca Merrill Groothius, *Discovering Biblical Equality: Complementarity Without Hierarchy* (Downers Grove, IL: InterVarsity Press, 2005); James R. Beck, ed., *Two Views on Women in Ministry*, rev. ed. (Grand Rapids, MI: Zondervan, 2005).

59. Kathleen Elkins, "20 Jobs That Are Dominated by Women," Business Insider, February 17, 2015, https://www.businessinsider .com/pink-collar-jobs-dominated-by-women-2015-2.

60. For examples, see Eric Mason, *Manhood Restored: How the Gospel Makes Men Whole* (Nashville: B&H Publishing, 2013); Wayne Grudem, *Biblical Foundations for Manhood and Womanhood* (Wheaton, IL: Crossway, 2002); John Piper and Wayne Grudem, eds., *Recovering Biblical Manhood and Womanhood: A Response to Evangelical Feminism* (Wheaton, IL: Crossway, 1991);

Andreas J. Köstenberger, *God's Design for Man and Woman: A Biblical-Theological Survey* (Wheaton, IL: Crossway, 2014).

61.   For the quote in context see u/JokeOfJudgementDay, "Andrea Dworkin's Quote About Wanting to See a Man Beaten. Does Anybody Have a Source? (details inside)," Reddit, August 20, 2013, https://www.reddit.com/r/SRSQuestions/comments/1krjac /andrea_dworkins_qoute_about_wanting_to_see_a_man/; see also Wikiquote, "Andrea Dworkin," last edited January 25, 2019, https:// en.wikiquote.org/wiki/Andrea_Dworkin.

CHAPTER 7: JEZEBEL AND THE WAR ON GENDER DISTINCTIONS

1.   Barack Obama, "Inaugural Address by President Barack Obama" (speech, Washington, DC, January 21, 2013), The White House, https://obamawhitehouse.archives.gov/the-press -office/2013/01/21/inaugural-address-president-barack-obama.

2.   Zeke J. Miller, "Axelrod: Obama Misled Nation When He Opposed Gay Marriage in 2008," *Time*, February 10, 2015, http:// time.com/3702584/gay-marriage-axelrod-obama/.

3.   Michael Brown, "Equivocating or Evolving, President Obama Is Wrong Either Way," Townhall, May 12, 2012, https:// townhall.com/columnists/michaelbrown/2012/05/12/equivocating -or-evolving-president-obama-is-wrong-either-way-n823824.

4.   James Risdon, "WATCH: Drag Queen Admits He's 'Grooming' Children at Story Hour Events," Life Site News, November 27, 2018, https://www.lifesitenews.com/news/watch -drag-queen-admits-hes-grooming-children-at-story-hour-events.

5.   For documentation, see Michael L. Brown, *A Queer Thing Happened to America: And What a Long Strange Trip It's Been* (Concord, NC: EqualTime Books, 2011); Michael L. Brown, *Outlasting the Gay Revolution: Where Homosexual Activism Is Really Going and How to Turn the Tide* (Washington, DC: WND Books, 2015). For additional articles search https://askdrbrown.org/ for relevant terms, including *homosexuality, gay, lesbian, transgender, queer,* and *LGBT.*

6.   Michael L. Brown, "What We Learned From the Arrest of Kim Davis," AskDrBrown, September 4, 2015, https://askdrbrown .org/library/what-we-learned-arrest-kim-davis.

7.   John Aravosis, "How Did the T Get in LGBT?," Salon, October 8, 2007, https://www.salon.com/2007/10/08/lgbt/.

8.   Michael L. Brown, "Thanks to 'Transgender Equality' Laws, Boys Are Now Sharing Girls' Locker Rooms," AskDrBrown, February 18, 2016, https://askdrbrown.org/library/thanks-transgender -equality-laws-boys-are-now-sharing-girls.

9.   Michael L. Brown, "Being Found Guilty of 'Transphobia' Could Cost You $250,000," AskDrBrown, January 6, 2016, https:// askdrbrown.org/library/being-found-guilty-transphobia-could-cost -you-250000; "NYC Commission on Human Rights Announces Strong Protections for City's Transgender and Gender Non-Conforming Communities in Housing, Employment and Public Spaces," The Official Website of the City of New York, December 21, 2015, https://www1.nyc.gov/office-of-the-mayor/news/961-15/ nyc-commission-human-rights-strong-protections-city-s -transgender-gender.

10.   Elise Schmelzer, "Colorado to Allow Use of X as Sex Identifier on Driver's Licenses Starting This Month," *Denver Post*, November 8, 2018, https://www.denverpost.com/2018/11/08 /colorado-drivers-license-x-gender/.

11.   Michael L. Brown, "Major Breaking News: Males Are Not Females," AskDrBrown, July 18, 2015, https://askdrbrown.org /library/major-breaking-news-males-are-not-females. For more about the eleven-year-old changing his birth certificate, see Ian Holliday, "11-Year-Old Transgender Girl 'Not Done Yet' After Changing Birth Certificate," CTV News Vancouver, updated July 23, 2014, https://bc.ctvnews.ca/11-year-old-transgender-girl -not-done-yet-after-changing-birth-certificate-1.1929208.

12.   NYC Health, "Health Department Announces New Law Offering Third Gender Category on Birth Certificates Takes Effect on Tuesday," Recent Press Releases, December 31, 2018, https:// www1.nyc.gov/site/doh/about/press/pr2018/pr104-18.page.

13.   Ruth Barrett, ed., *Female Erasure: What You Need To Know About Gender Politics' War on Women, the Female Sex and*

Human Rights (Pacific Palisades, CA: Tidal Time Publishing, 2016). The anthology includes forty-eight contributors who "celebrate female embodiment while exploring deeper issues of misogyny, violence, and sexism disguised today as progressive politics." (See "About the Book," Female Erasure, accessed April 7, 2019, https://www.femaleerasure.com/.)

14.　Michael L. Brown, "Sign This Petition and Proclaim That Biology Is Not Bigotry," AskDrBrown, December 10, 2018, https://askdrbrown.org/library/sign-petition-and-proclaim-biology-not-bigotry. Specifically, see "The Assault on Gender and Gender Studies," American Association of University Professors, November 2018, https://www.aaup.org/assault-gender-and-gender-studies.

15.　Jessi Hempel, "My Brother's Pregnancy and the Making of a New American Family," *Time*, September 12, 2016, http://time.com/4475634/trans-man-pregnancy-evan/.

16.　Sanchez Manning, "Eight-Year-Old Pupils to Be Told 'Boys Can Have Periods Too' Under New Sex Education Lessons Guidelines," *Daily Mail*, updated December 16, 2018, https://www.dailymail.co.uk/news/article-6500231/Eight-year-old-pupils-told-boys-periods-new-sex-education-guidelines.html.

17.　Barb Burdge, "Bending Gender, Ending Gender: Theoretical Foundations for Social Work Practice With the Transgender Community," *Social Work* 52, no. 3 (July 2007). Abstract available at https://www.questia.com/library/journal/1G1-168292343/bending-gender-ending-gender-theoretical-foundations.

18.　Barrett, ed., *Female Erasure*, xxxiii.

19.　Wikipedia, s.v. "The Feminists," last edited March 26, 2018, https://en.wikipedia.org/wiki/The_Feminists. The group split from NOW, the National Organization of Women, in 1968.

20.　Wikipedia, s.v. "The Feminists."

21.　For some of the dynamics involved, see Peter LaBarbera, "Lesbian Couple, Both Pregnant With Boys, Plans to Raise 'Feminist Men,'" Life Site News, March 29, 2017, https://www.lifesitenews.com/news/lesbian-couple-both-pregnant-with-boys-to-raise-feminist-men.

22.　Rob Schwarzwalder and Natasha Tax, "How Fatherlessness Impacts Early Sexual Activity, Teen Pregnancy, and Sexual Abuse,"

Family Research Council, December 2015, https://downloads. frc.org/EF/EF15L32.pdf; "The Consequences of Fatherlessness," Fathers.com, accessed March 18, 2019, http://fathers.com/statistics -and-research/the-consequences-of-fatherlessness/2/.

23.   For a different perspective see Warren Thockmorton, "Does Father Absence Cause Homosexuality?," Crosswalk.com, November 24, 2008, https://www.crosswalk.com/blogs/dr-warren -throckmorton/does-father-absence-cause-homosexuality-11596147. html. For a pro-and-con of both perspectives see "Can a Child's Relationship With His or Her Parents Cause Homosexuality?," ProCon.org, updated March 19, 2008, https://borngay.procon.org /view.answers.php?questionID=000027.

24.   Joseph Nicolosi, "Fathers of Male Homosexuals: A Collective Clinical Profile," JosephNicolosi.com, accessed April 8, 2019, https://www.josephnicolosi.com/collection/2015/5/30/fathers-of -male-homosexuals-a-collective-clinical-profile, second emphasis added.

25.   Walter E. Williams, "The True Black Tragedy: Illegitimacy Rate of Nearly 75%," CNSNews.com, May 19, 2015, http://www .cnsnews.com/commentary/walter-e-williams/true-black-tragedy -illegitimacy-rate-nearly-75.

26.   Williams, "The True Black Tragedy."

27.   Williams, "The True Black Tragedy."

28.   Brandon Ambrosino, "Why Some Black Men Prefer the Down Low and What It Says About the Black Church in America," *Washington Post*, September 4, 2015, https://www.washingtonpost .com/national/religion/why-some-black-men-prefer-the-down-low -and-what-it-says-about-the-black-church-in-america/2015/09/04 /59788754-533b-11e5-b225-90edbd49f362_story.html.

29.   "HIV and African American Gay and Bisexual Men," Centers for Disease Control and Prevention, updated March 19, 2019, https://www.cdc.gov/hiv/group/msm/bmsm.html.

30.   "CDC Fact Sheet: HIV Gay and Bisexual Men," Centers for Disease Control and Prevention, February 2017, https://www.cdc .gov/nchhstp/newsroom/docs/factsheets/cdc-msm-508.pdf.

31.   For example, see David Masci, "5 Facts About the Religious Lives of African Americans," Pew Research Center, February 7,

2018, http://www.pewresearch.org/fact-tank/2018/02/07/5-facts
-about-the-religious-lives-of-african-americans/; and David Masci,
Besheer Mohamed, and Gregory A. Smith, "Black Americans Are
More Likely Than Overall Public to be Christian, Protestant," Pew
Research Center, April 23, 2018, http://www.pewresearch.org/fact
-tank/2018/04/23/black-americans-are-more-likely-than-overall
-public-to-be-christian-protestant/.

32.   According to the Maafa21 website, which features a pro-
vocative documentary called *Black Genocide in 21st Century
America*, "They were stolen from their homes, locked in chains
and taken across an ocean. And for more than 200 years, their
blood and sweat would help to build the richest and most powerful nation the world has ever known. But when slavery ended,
their welcome was over. America's wealthy elite had decided it was
time for them to disappear and they were not particular about
how it might be done. What you are about to see is that the plan
these people set in motion 150 years ago is still being carried out
today. So don't think that this is history. It is not. It is happening
right here, and it's happening right now." See Homepage, Maafa21,
accessed April 7, 2019, http://www.maafa21.com/.

33.   Homepage, Blackgenocide.org, accessed April 7, 2019,
http://blackgenocide.org/?fbclid=IwAR0DxaHfopxIytKvMQYE3BD
unwAM2LYnewPhvdwOwRrDSkwLKeZjwpXp8r4/. For a non-
conservative perspective, see P. R. Lockhart, "'Abortion as Black
Genocide': Inside the Black Anti-abortion Movement," Vox, January
19, 2018, https://www.vox.com/identities/2018/1/19/16906928
/black-anti-abortion-movement-yoruba-richen-medical-racism.

34.   National Right to Life Committee, Inc., *The State of Abortion in the United States*.

35.   Schwarzwalder and Tax, "How Fatherlessness Impacts
Early Sexual Activity, Teen Pregnancy, and Sexual Abuse,"
emphasis added.

36.   Dallin H. Oaks, "Truth and the Plan," The Church of Jesus
Christ of Latter-Day Saints, October 2018, https://www.lds
.org/general-conference/2018/10/truth-and-the-plan?lang=eng.
For this, Oaks was included as one of "The 10 Biggest Homophobes and Transphobes of 2018." See Trudy Ring, "The 10 Biggest

Homophobes and Transphobes of 2018," *Advocate*, December 24, 2018, https://www.advocate.com/news/2018/12/24/10-biggest -homophobes-and-transphobes-2018#media-gallery-media-2.

37.   Francis Schaeffer, *The Complete Works of Francis A. Schaeffer: A Christian Worldview*, vol. 1 (Wheaton, IL, Crossway Books, 1982), 37, https://books.google.com/books?id=RPYorgYh UZsC&pg.

38.   Michael L. Brown, "Why LGBT's War on Gender Must Be Resisted," AskDrBrown, December 10, 2014, https://askdrbrown .org/library/why-lgbts-war-gender-must-be-resisted.

39.   Pacific Justice Institute, "School Stirs Controversy With 'Genderbread,' Sex Checklists," press release, December 8, 2014, https://www.pacificjustice.org/press-releases/school-stirs -controversy-with-genderbread-sex-checklists.

40.   Michael Gryboski, "Former Lesbian Candidate for United Methodist Ordination Undergoing 'Gender Transition,'" *Christian Post*, December 5, 2014, https://webcache.googleusercontent.com /search?q=cache:RFwi8-g_FboJ:https://www.christianpost.com /news/former-lesbian-candidate-for-united-methodist-ordination -undergoing-gender-transition.html+&cd=1&hl=en&ct=clnk&gl=us.

41.   Brown, "Why LGBT's War on Gender Must Be Resisted."

42.   Facebook's gender options are now simply male, female, and custom (fill in the blank).

43.   Special thanks to Caleb H. Price for researching and developing this list of terms, which appears in Brown, *A Queer Thing Happened to America*, 592.

44.   Diane Ehrensaft, *Gender Born, Gender Made: Raising Healthy Gender-Nonconforming Children* (New York, The Experiment, 2011), 228, https://books.google.com/books?id=4epYo0o sBzcC&pg.

45.   Margot Adler, "Young People Push Back Against Gender Categories," NPR, July 16, 2013, https://www.npr.org/templates /story/story.php?storyId=202729367. See also Michael L. Brown, "'Call Me Tractor,'" AskDrBrown, February 18, 2014, https://ask drbrown.org/library/call-me-tractor.

46. Michael Brown, "Lies About Gender and Marriage," *Decision*, March 2017, https://billygraham.org/decision-magazine /march-2017/54136-2/.

47. For an illustrated video see AskDrBrown, "Stephen Colbert Proves My Point About the Slippery Slope," YouTube, October 2, 2015, https://www.youtube.com/watch?v =WKgTS3b3ZTI/.

48. In the past I have seen a quote close to this attributed to G. K. Chesterton, but these exact words are those of Burnham. See Walter Dean Burnham, "Democracy and the Court," *Commonweal*, July 24, 1964, 503, http://www.unz.com/print/Commonweal -1964jul24-00499/Contents/. For a Chesterton quote that is close, see G. K. Chesterton, *The Thing* (1929), http://www.gkc.org.uk/gkc /books/The_Thing.txt.

49. Bill Muehlenberg, "The Terrorism of Trans Tyranny," CultureWatch, December 13, 2018, https://billmuehlenberg.com /2018/12/13/the-terrorism-of-trans-tyranny/.

50. Victoria Cobb, "BREAKING: Teacher Refused to Lie About Gender—Fired From West Point High School Tonight," Family Foundation, December 6, 2018, http://www.familyfoundation.org /blog/breaking-teacher-refused-to-lie-about-gender-fired-from-west -point-high-school-tonight.

51. "Law Professor Threatened With Rape and Murder After Saying, 'A Woman Is Defined by Law as Biological Not Psychological,'" Caldron Pool, December 6, 2018, http://caldronpool.com /law-professor-threatened-with-rape-and-murder-after-saying-a -woman-is-defined-by-law-as-biological-not-psychological/.

52. Jonathon Van Maren, "Canadian Man Claiming to Be 'Female' Sues 16 Women for Refusing to Wax His Genitals," Life Site News, November 12, 2018, https://www.lifesitenews.com/blogs /canadian-man-claiming-to-be-female-sues-16-women-for-refusing -to-wax-his-ge.

53. Lisa Bourne, "6-Year-Old Boy Forced to Live as a Girl While Mom Threatens Dad for Not Going Along," Life Site News, November 28, 2018, https://www.lifesitenews.com/news/6-year-old -boy-forced-to-live-as-a-girl-while-mom-threatens-dad-for-not-goi.

54.　Michael Gryboski, "Mom Appeals After Losing Against School That Gave Son Transgender Medical Treatments Without Her Permission," *Christian Post*, August 4, 2017, https://www.christianpost.com/news/mom-appeals-after-losing-against-school-that-gave-son-transgender-medical-treatments-without-her-permission.html.

55.　Muehlenberg, "The Terrorism of Trans Tyranny."

56.　Dennis Prager, "Feminization of America Is Bad for the World," *National Review*, November 3, 2015, https://www.nationalreview.com/2015/11/gender-differences-are-important/.

57.　Prager, "Feminization of America Is Bad for the World."

58.　Prager, "Feminization of America Is Bad for the World." For some general reflections on the differences between males and females see "Key Differences Between Male and Female," Focus on the Family, 2015, https://www.focusonthefamily.com/family-q-and-a/sexuality/key-differences-between-male-and-female; cf. Steven E. Rhoads, *Taking Sex Differences Seriously* (San Francisco: Encounter Books, 2004). For a practical study see Glenn T. Stanton, *Secure Daughters, Confident Sons: How Parents Guide Their Children into Authentic Masculinity and Femininity* (Colorado Springs, CO: Multnomah Books, 2013).

59.　George Gillett, "We Shouldn't Fight for 'Gender Equality'. We Should Fight to Abolish Gender," *New Statesman*, October 2, 2014, https://www.newstatesman.com/society/2014/10/we-shouldn-t-fight-gender-equality-we-should-fight-abolish-gender.

60.　Gillett, "We Shouldn't Fight for 'Gender Equality.'"

61.　AskDrBrown, "Can You Be Gay and Christian?," YouTube, May 2, 2018, https://www.youtube.com/watch?v=5l_GY6mXgQg&lc.

62.　See Michael L. Brown, "Does the Younger Generation Want to Burn Us at the Stake?," AskDrBrown, August 22, 2018, https://askdrbrown.org/library/does-younger-generation-want-burn-us-stake. This comment has been deleted.

CHAPTER 8: JEZEBEL AND THE RISE OF WITCHCRAFT

1.　　Sangeeta Singh-Kurtz and Dan Kopf, "The US Witch Population Has Seen an Astronomical Rise," Quartzy, October 4, 2018, https://qz.com/quartzy/1411909/the-explosive-growth-of-witches-wiccans-and-pagans-in-the-us/.

2.　　Brett Tingley, "Surveys Find Witchcraft Is on the Rise Across America," Mysterious Universe, October 10, 2018, https://mysteriousuniverse.org/2018/10/surveys-find-witchcraft-is-on-the-rise-across-america/.

3.　　Calvin Freiburger, "Report: Witchcraft Rising in US as Christianity Declines," Life Site News, October 11, 2018, https://www.lifesitenews.com/news/report-witchcraft-rising-in-us-as-christianity-declines.

4.　　Benjamin Fearnow, "Number of Witches Rises Dramatically Across U.S. as Millennials Reject Christianity."

5.　　Alison Lesley, "Witches Outnumbers Presbyterians Among U.S. Millennials," World Religion News, October 11, 2018, https://www.worldreligionnews.com/religion-news/witches-outnumbers-presbyterians-among-u-s-millennials.

6.　　Christine Rousselle, "Number of Americans Who Say They Are Witches Is on the Rise," Catholic News Agency, October 30, 2018, https://www.catholicnewsagency.com/news/more-than-a-million-americans-say-they-are-witches-31750.

7.　　Kari Paul, "Why Millennials Are Ditching Religion for Witchcraft and Astrology," MarketWatch, October 31, 2018, https://www.marketwatch.com/story/why-millennials-are-ditching-religion-for-witchcraft-and-astrology-2017-10-20.

8.　　Christina Marfice, "There Are Now More Practicing Witches in the U.S. Than Ever Before," Scary Mommy, November 19, 2018, https://www.scarymommy.com/witches-rising-numbers/.

9.　　Michael Snyder, "The Fastest Growing Religion in America Is Witchcraft," The Truth, October 30, 2013, http://thetruthwins.com/archives/the-fastest-growing-religion-in-america-is-witchcraft.

10.　　Pottermore News Team, "500 Million Harry Potter Books Have Now Been Sold Worldwide," Pottermore, February 1, 2018,

https://www.pottermore.com/news/500-million
-harry-potter-books-have-now-been-sold-worldwide.

11.   James White (@DrOakley1689), "It is very hard not to see
a strong spirit of deception and delusion working in this culture—
we murder our babies, destroy the gift of marriage, even mutilate
young children all in service to the god of human autonomy. But,
the judgment is just," Twitter, December 16, 2018, 6:44 a.m., https://
twitter.com/DrOakley1689/status/1074314225617559557. Dr. White
was interacting with my comments that "I took time last night to
exchange scores (or hundreds?) of tweets with so-called 'progressive'
Christians and their friends (including atheists). Not ONE gave me
a single scripture to support their views or refute mine. Their argument is with God and His Word, not with me," and, "Aside from
always trying to reach out, I wanted to make last night an extended,
teachable moment. In that respect, sadly, the mission was more
than accomplished. A whole lot was revealed from the anti-Word
side." See Dr. Michael L. Brown (@DrMichaelLBrown), "I took time
last night to exchange scores (or hundreds?) of tweets with so-called
'progressive' Christians and their friends (including atheists)…,"
Twitter, December 16, 2018, 6:32 a.m., https://twitter.com/Dr
MichaelLBrown/status/1074311293211959297; Dr. Michael L. Brown
(@DrMichaelLBrown), "Aside from always trying to reach out, I
wanted to make last night an extended, teachable moment…"
Twitter, December 16, 2018, 6:35 a.m., https://twitter.com
/DrMichaelLBrown/status/1074312088733081600. The lengthy
exchange was initiated by an attack on me by "progressive" pastor
John Pavlovitz. See John Pavlovitz (@johnpavlovitz), "When hope-
lessly phobic people of faith like @DrMichaelLBrown claim
that God is against 'homosexual practice.' #ThatsNotAThing,"
Twitter, December 15, 2018, https://twitter.com/johnpavlovitz/
status/1074102401358069760.

12.   Mark Richardson, "Yoko Ono," Pitchfork, February 12,
2007, https://pitchfork.com/features/interview/6541-yoko-ono/.
Interestingly, people didn't think she should release the song "Yes,
I'm a Witch" when she first wrote it in 1974, but within a generation it draws no outrage.

13.   Finn Mackay, *Radical Feminism: Feminist Activism in Movement* (Hampshire, UK: Palgrave Macmillan, 2015), 1, https://books.google.com/books?id=X9e_CQAAQBAJ&q.

14.   The graphic can be found at Finn Mackay, "Raising Children Without Gender Stereotypes," Let Toys Be Toys, September 21, 2018, http://lettoysbetoys.org.uk/raising-children-without-gender-stereotypes/.

15.   Homepage, Finn Mackay, accessed February 5, 2019, https://finnmackay.wordpress.com/.

16.   Traister, *Good and Mad*, ix.

17.   Lily Burana, "2018 Was the Year American Women Embraced Their Inner Witch," HuffPost, December 23, 2018, https://www.huffingtonpost.com/entry/opinion-witchcraft-women-2018_us_5c1d227ce4b0407e907a9c7f.

18.   Burana, "2018 Was the Year American Women Embraced Their Inner Witch."

19.   Burana, "2018 Was the Year American Women Embraced Their Inner Witch."

20.   For a relevant academic study see Laisa Schweigert, "W.I.T.C.H. and Witchcraft in Radical Feminist Activism," (master's thesis, Arizona State University, 2018), https://repository.asu.edu/items/49239.

21.   Peter J. Reilly, "Lesbians Want a Church of Their Own and IRS Approves," *Forbes*, August 3, 2018, https://www.forbes.com/sites/peterjreilly/2018/08/03/lesbians-want-a-church-of-their-own-and-irs-approves/#7bc0de2521c2; Peter J. Reilly, "Why Gender-Critical Radical Feminists Might Want a Church and Why IRS Approved," *Forbes*, August 12, 2018, https://www.forbes.com/sites/peterjreilly/2018/08/12/why-gender-critical-radical-feminists-might-want-a-church-and-why-irs-approved/#67e71d94e4e0. The name of the "church" contained a female-referenced expletive; hence its relevance here.

22.   Dr. Finn Mackay (@Finn_Mackay), "Exciting! Had my paper on #butch #lesbian identity accepted for the BSA Conference next year…" Twitter, November 24, 2017, 9:07 a.m., https://twitter.com/Finn_Mackay/status/934106189943705600.

23.   Finn Mackay, "Whose Afraid of Female Masculinity?," August 20, 2018, https://finnmackay.wordpress.com/articles/whose -afraid-of-female-masculinity/. In the article she notes, "The idea of butch masculinity is, of course, not new, and the topics of female masculinity and lesbian gender run through many classics on any Gender Studies bookshelf or University programme."

24.   See also Cheryl K. Chumley, "Satanists and Planned Parenthood—a Match Made in Hell," Washington Times, September 13, 2017, https://www.washingtontimes.com/news/2017/ sep/13/satanists-and-planned-parenthood-match-made-hell/.

25.   Jenni Fink, "Witches Hex Brett Kavanaugh, Hope to Cause Suffering to GOP, Donald Trump," *Newsweek*, October 22, 2018, https://www.newsweek.com/witches-hex-brett-kavanaugh-hope -cause-suffering-gop-donald-trump-1181543.

26.   Fink, "Witches Hex Brett Kavanaugh."

27.   Linda Harvey, "Witches at the Abortion Clinic 'Blessing,'" Mission: America, November 10, 2018, https://www.mission america.com/article/witches-at-the-abortion-clinic-blessing/.

28.   Tara Isabella Burton, "Each Month, Thousands of Witches Cast a Spell Against Donald Trump," Vox, updated October 30, 2017, https://www.vox.com/2017/6/20/15830312/magicresistance -restance-witches-magic-spell-to-bind-donald-trump-mememagic.

29.   Local 12, "The Cooler: Real School of Witchcraft and Wizardry," YouTube, December 9, 2014, https://www.youtube.com /watch?v=Ni88bBUd32I; Kim Renfro and Jacob Shamsian, "$400 Gets Any Muggle Into This 'Harry Potter'-Inspired Wizarding School to Practice Magic," Insider, September 22, 2016, https:// www.thisisinsider.com/harry-potter-real-wizard-school -poland-2016-9.

30.   Michael Snyder, "What's Behind the Seemingly Unrelenting Rise of Satanism?," Charisma News, January 19, 2017, https://www.charismanews.com/opinion/62500-what-s-behind -the-seemingly-unrelenting-rise-of-satanism.

31.   "Rise of Satanism Another Sign of 'America's Fall From God,'" WND.com, September 27, 2016, https://www.wnd. com/2016/09/rise-of-satanism-another-sign-of-americas-fall-from -god/.

32.   Michael Gryboski, "American Society 'Submerged' in the Occult, Says Ex-Satanist," *Christian Post*, March 8, 2013, https://www.christianpost.com/news/american-society-submerged-in-the-occult-says-ex-satanist.html.

33.   Iben Thranholm, "What the [Expletive]? Satan Worship on Rise in America," RT, August 29, 2016, https://www.rt.com/op-ed/357523-what-hell-satan-worship-america/.

34.   Sheila Flynn, "The Rise of Satanism in America: How Members of the Satanic Temple Focus on Activism, Religious Pluralism and Social Diversity but Surprisingly NOT devil Worship— As Leaders Are Plagued by Death Threats and Infighting," *Daily Mail*, updated January 22, 2019, https://www.dailymail.co.uk/news/article-6616577/The-rise-Satanism-America-members-dont-ACTUALLY-worship-devil-push-activism.html.

35.   Richard Kyle, "The Occult Roars Back: Its Modern Resurgence," *Direction* 29, no. 2 (Fall 2000): 91–99, http://www.directionjournal.org/29/2/occult-roars-back-its-modern-resurgence.html.

36.   Kyle, "The Occult Roars Back."

37.   Gryboski, "American Society 'Submerged' in the Occult."

38.   Patti Armstrong, "US Exorcists: Demonic Activity on the Rise," *National Catholic Register*, March 11, 2017, http://www.ncregister.com/daily-news/us-exorcists-demonic-activity-on-the-rise.

39.   "0.0% of Icelanders 25 Years or Younger Believe God Created the World, Poll Reveals," *Iceland Magazine*, January 14, 2016, https://icelandmag.is/article/00-icelanders-25-years-or-younger-believe-god-created-world-poll-reveals.

40.   Rodney Stark, *The Triumph of Faith: Why the World Is More Religious Than Ever* (Wilmington, DE: ISI Books, 2015), 6, https://books.google.com/books?id=owS6CgAAQBAJ&q. For further excerpts and related discussion see Brown, *Saving a Sick America*, 50–52.

41.   Paul Nowak, "The Seven Most Popular G. K. Chesterton Quotes He Never Said," The Federalist, May 6, 2014, http://thefederalist.com/2014/05/06/the-seven-most-popular-g-k-chesterton-quotes-he-never-said/.

42.   Alex Mar, "Witches of America: How I Became Immersed in a Growing Movement," *The Guardian*, October 29, 2016, https://

www.theguardian.com/lifeandstyle/2016/oct/29/witches-of
-america-alex-mar-pagan-witchcraft.

43.   Mar, "Witches of America."

44.   Mar, "Witches of America."

45.   Mar, "Witches of America."

46.   Merritt Tierce, "'Witches of America,' by Alex Mar," *New
York Times*, October 27, 2015, https://www.nytimes.com/2015
/11/01/books/review/witches-of-america-by-alex-mar.html.

47.   Mar, "Witches of America."

48.   Michael L. Brown, "Why Can't You Be a Christian Witch?,"
AskDrBrown, October 22, 2018, https://askdrbrown.org/library
/why-can%E2%80%99t-you-be-christian-witch.

CHAPTER 9: JEZEBEL AND THE SILENCING OF THE PROPHETS

1.   Note that in 1 Kings 22:11–12, the false prophet Zedekiah,
together with the rest of the prophets, claims to be prophesying in
Yahweh's name, most likely in response to Jehoshaphat's words. See
also 1 Kings 22:24.

2.   Pesikta Rabbati 26:13, Sefaria, accessed April 8, 2019,
https://www.sefaria.org/Pesikta_Rabbati.26?lang=bi.

3.   Abraham J. Heschel, *The Prophets* (New York: Perennial
Classics, 2001), 19, https://www.amazon.com/Prophets-Perennial
-Classics-Abraham-Heschel/dp/0060936991.

4.   Heschel, *The Prophets*, 12.

5.   Excerpted and reorganized from Leonard Ravenhill, "Picture of a Prophet," 1994, http://www.ravenhill.org/prophet.htm.

6.   Michael L. Brown, *Playing With Holy Fire* (Lake Mary, FL:
Charisma House, 2018); Jeremiah Johnson, *Cleansing and Igniting
the Prophetic: An Urgent Wake-Up Call* (Shippensburg, PA: Destiny Image, 2018).

7.   The Daily Wire, "Sunday Special Ep 29: Pastor John
MacArthur," YouTube, December 2, 2018, https://www.youtube
.com/watch?v=F-ofKxfYqGw.

8.   Michael L. Brown (@DrMichaelLBrown), "'If you try to
develop a kind of Christianity that's inoffensive, it's not Christianity.' (Pastor John MacArthur) Well said!," Twitter, December 2,

2018, 8:17 a.m., https://twitter.com/DrMichaelLBrown/status /1069264226462679041.

9.   For hundreds of years the English-speaking church has wrongly called the Letter of Jacob the Letter of James, as James in Greek is actually Jacob. I believe it is high time to correct this error and attribute this epistle to the apostle Jacob instead of the apostle James. For more information on how Jacob became James, see Michael L. Brown, "Recovering the Lost Letter of Jacob," Charisma News, February 20, 2019, https://www.charismanews.com /opinion/38591-recovering-the-lost-letter-of-jacob.

10.   Michael L. Brown (@DrMichaelLBrown), "Do you want to be a hero to sinners?...," Twitter, December 15, 2018, 8:46 p.m., https://twitter.com/DrMichaelLBrown/status/1074163805557612546.

11.   AskDrBrown, "Why Don't More Pastors Speak Out?," YouTube, November 7, 2018, https://www.youtube.com/watch?v =gOPB2hbrqsM.

12.   Michael L. Brown (@DrMichaelLBrown), "There was a time in America when Christian leaders were expected to speak out against sin...," Twitter, December 9, 2018, 4:28 p.m., https://twitter .com/DrMichaelLBrown/status/1071924600735444999.

13.   Michael L. Brown (@DrMichaelLBrown), "The gospel of Jesus: If you want to be My disciple, deny yourself, take up the cross, and follow Me...," Twitter, December 10, 2018, 9:15 p.m., https://twitter.com/DrMichaelLBrown/status/1072359093 938085888.

14.   David R. Reagan, "David Wilkerson: America's Prophet of Destruction," *Lamplighter* 36, no. 5 (September/October 2015), 4, http://lamblion.com/xfiles/publications/magazines/Lamplighter _SepOct15_Wilkerson.pdf.

15.   Reagan, "David Wilkerson."

16.   Peter Marshall, "Trial by Fire" (sermon, St. Charles Presbyterian Church, New Orleans, LA, March 11, 1944), accessed at Sermon Library, "Trial by Fire by Peter Marshall," YouTube, October 1, 2017, https://www.youtube.com/watch?v=WbXHlunwEoQ.

17.   Marshall, "Trial by Fire."

18.   Marshall, "Trial by Fire."

19.   100huntley, "'Billy Graham TV Appearance Montage'—
TRUTH TO GO with Franklin Graham," YouTube, November 10,
2011, https://www.youtube.com/watch?v=ka4nxveH8pE.

CHAPTER 10: JEZEBEL, JEHU, AND DONALD TRUMP

1.   Mike Storti, "Jezebel—The Original Feminist," Bible
Watchman, accessed April 8, 2019, http://biblewatchman.com
/jezebel.htm. To be clear, Pastor Storti and I would strongly disagree
on a number of important issues, including his view that the King
James Version is "the infallibly preserved Word of God." (See Mike
Storti, "Preaching the Infallibly, Preserved Word of God, The King
James Version," Bible Watchman, accessed April 8, 2019, http://www
.biblewatchman.com/.) He is also strongly anti-Charismatic. (See
Mike Storti, "The Deceiving, Charismatic Beasts," Bible Watchman,
accessed April 9, 2019, http://biblewatchman.com/charismatic.htm.)
I point this out not to differ with him here but to make clear that he
would not endorse my position on other matters.

2.   Storti, "Jezebel."

3.   This is one of her most famous quotes: "You cannot have
maternal health without reproductive health. And reproductive
health includes contraception and family planning and access
to legal, safe abortion." (See Hillary Rodham Clinton, "Remarks
With G-8 Foreign Ministers After Their Ministerial Meetings," US
Department of State, March 30, 2010, https://2009-2017.state.gov/
secretary/20092013clinton/rm/2010/03/139287.htm.) See also Alex-
andra DeSanctis, "Why Hillary Clinton Deserves Planned Parenthood's Award," National Review, April 17, 2017, https://www
.nationalreview.com/2017/04/hillary-clinton-planned-parenthoods
-appalling-champion/.

4.   Joel B. Pollak, "Pollak: Donald Trump, the Biblical King
Jehu, and the Unfinished Border Wall," Breitbart, December 15,
2018, https://www.breitbart.com/politics/2018/12/15/pollak-donald-
trump-the-biblical-king-jehu-and-the-unfinished-border-wall
-2-kings/.

5.   Pollak, "Pollak."

6.   Jonathan Cahn, *The Paradigm: The Ancient Blueprint That Holds the Mystery of Our Times* (Lake Mary, FL: FrontLine, 2017).

7.   Quoted in Nathan Jones, "A Biblical Blueprint for America: Jehu as Trump's Paradigm," *Christ in Prophecy Journal* (blog), November 8, 2018, http://christinprophecyblog.org/2018/11/a -biblical-blueprint-for-america-jehu-as-trumps-paradigm/.

8.   Jones, "A Biblical Blueprint for America."

9.   Jones, "A Biblical Blueprint for America."

10.   Jones, "A Biblical Blueprint for America."

11.   Andrei Shary, "Femen Leader Explains Why She Accosted Putin," *The Atlantic*, April 10, 2013, https://www.theatlantic.com /international/archive/2013/04/femen-leader-explains-why-she -accosted-putin/274872/.

12.   Michael L. Brown, *Donald Trump Is Not My Savior: An Evangelical Leader Speaks His Mind About the Man He Supports as President* (Shippensburg, PA: Destiny Image, 2018). In the book I chronicle my views about Trump from August 2015 until August 2018, raising serious questions about Evangelical support for the president, explaining why I once opposed him but ultimately voted for him, and offering guidelines for Evangelicals and politics for the years to come.

13.   Chris Riotta, "Donald Trump Is Reckless, Erratic and Incompetent, According to Business Leaders Around the World," *Newsweek*, June 23, 2017, https://www.newsweek.com/donald -trump-reckless-erratic-dictator-business-leaders-say-cnbc-survey -628569.

14.   Todd Spangler, "Majority of Voters Think Trump Is Reckless, Poll Says," *Detroit Free Press*, October 25, 2017, https://www .freep.com/story/news/local/michigan/2017/10/25/trump-reckless -poll-says/798438001/.

15.   Rebecca Savransky, "Poll: Majorities Think Trump Is Reckless, Profane and Sexist," *The Hill*, January 28, 2018, https://thehill .com/homenews/administration/371082-poll-majorities-think -trump-is-reckless-profane-and-sexist.

16.   Dana Milbank, "Trump's Not a Liar. He's a Madman," *Washington Post*, May 29, 2018, https://www.washingtonpost.com

/opinions/trump-doesnt-lie-he-does-something-worse/2018/05/29 /fdd89d30-6372-11e8-99d2-0d678ec08c2f_story.html.

17. Tim Stanley, "War of Words: Trump, Visionary or Madman?," *The Telegraph*, May 25, 2018, https://www.telegraph .co.uk/news/2018/05/25/war-words-trump-visionary-madman/.

18. Chris Cillizza, "A Virginia Democrat Called Trump a 'Narcissistic Maniac.' And He's Not the Liberal in the Race!," CNN, updated June 5, 2017, https://www.cnn.com/2017/06/05/politics /tom-perriello-ralph-northam-virginia/index.html.

19. See again Burton, "Each Month, Thousands of Witches Cast a Spell Against Donald Trump."

20. Rachel Ray, "Witchcraft Moves to the Mainstream in America as Christianity Declines—and Has Trump in Its Sights," *The Telegraph*, December 21, 2018, https://www.telegraph.co.uk /news/2018/12/21/witchcraft-moves-mainstream-america -christianity-declines/.

21. For examples, see Claire Cohen, "Donald Trump Sexism Tracker: Every Offensive Comment in One Place," *The Telegraph*, July 14, 2017, https://www.telegraph.co.uk/women/politics/donald -trump-sexism-tracker-every-offensive-comment-in-one-place/.

22. Again, these are questions that I address in *Donald Trump Is Not My Savior*.

23. Cohen, "Donald Trump Sexism Tracker."

24. Don Reisinger, "Michelle Obama Calls Donald Trump a 'Misogynist' Who Incited 'Kooks' in New Memoir," *Fortune*, November 9, 2018, http://fortune.com/2018/11/09/michelle-obama -donald-trump/.

25. Gina Mei, "61 Celebrities Who Are Not Fans of President Trump, Nope, Not Even a Little Bit," *Cosmopolitan*, February 10, 2017, https://www.cosmopolitan.com/politics/a8684320/celebrities -hate-president-trump/.

26. Ronaldo ampao, "Madonna's Women's March Speech January 21st, 2017," YouTube, June 9, 2017, https://www.youtube.com /watch?v=THL-cEPHm3s&t=54s. See also Jayme Deerwester, "The Most Memorable Quotes From the Women's March on Washington," *USA Today*, updated January 21, 2017, https://www

.usatoday.com/story/life/entertainthis/2017/01/21/most-memorable
-quotes-womens-march-washington/96890596/.

27.   Holmes, *The Book of Jezebel*, 184–185.

28.   Traister, *Good and Mad*, xvii–xviii.

29.   See for yourself here: CNN, "Anti-Kavanaugh Protesters
Bang on the Doors of the Supreme Court," YouTube, October 6,
2018, https://www.youtube.com/watch?v=IRnmnxVtDqg. Kavanaugh, of course, was himself accused of sexual misconduct and
abuse but with no corroborating evidence of any kind.

30.   *Good and Mad.* Searched on Kindle.

31.   See Michael Brown, "Seven Things the Donald Trump
Wrecking Ball Has Exposed in Our Culture," The Stream, October
13, 2016, https://stream.org/seven-things-the-donald-trump
-wrecking-ball-has-exposed-in-our-culture/; and Michael Brown,
"Donald Trump and the Principle of Divine Upheaval," Townhall,
November 28, 2017, https://townhall.com/columnists/michael
brown/2017/11/28/donald-trump-and-the-principle-of-divine
-upheaval-n2415167.

32.   Daniel Block, "Is Trump Our Cyrus? The Old Testament
Case for Yes and No," *Christianity Today*, October 29, 2018, https://
www.christianitytoday.com/ct/2018/october-web-only/donald
-trump-cyrus-prophecy-old-testament.html.

33.   Matt Broomfield, "Women's March Against Donald Trump
Is the Largest Day of Protests in US History, Say Political Scientists," *The Independent*, January 23, 2017, https://www.independent
.co.uk/news/world/americas/womens-march-anti-donald-trump
-womens-rights-largest-protest-demonstration-us-history-political
-a7541081.html.

34.   Broomfield, "Women's March Against Donald Trump Is
the Largest Day of Protests in US History, Say Political Scientists."

35.   Bella Abzug et al., "Guiding Vision and Definition of Principles," Women's March on Washington, accessed April 8, 2019,
https://web.archive.org/web/20170207085559/https://static1.square
space.com/static/584086c7be6594762f5ec56e/t/58796773414fb52
b57e20794/1484351351914/WMW+Guiding+Vision+%26+Definition
+of+Principles.pdf.

36.   Abzug et al., "Guiding Vision and Definition of Principles."

37. Abzug et al., "Guiding Vision and Definition of Principles."

38. Abzug et al., "Guiding Vision and Definition of Principles."

39. Abzug et al., "Guiding Vision and Definition of Principles."

40. For more on the rise of witchcraft in America see chapter 8.

CHAPTER 11: HOW TO DEFEAT JEZEBEL IN YOUR PERSONAL LIFE

1. It is used in modern Hebrew for *husband* but *not* in that context in the sense of master or lord.

2. Cf. 2 Samuel 2:8 with 1 Chronicles 8:33, speaking of the same person; Ish and Esh are virtually identical. The same thing apparently happened with Jonathan's son Mephibosheth, which means from the mouth of shame. Originally the name was apparently Merib-Baal, from the mouth of ba'al, which could have easily referred to the Lord.

3. Another way to understand the Hebrew is that it means "no exaltation" or "no honor." See "Jezebel Meaning," Abarim Publications, updated November 21, 2017, http://www.abarim-publications.com/Meaning/Jezebel.html#.XBnFKVxKiF4.

4. Note that the word for *dung* here is the Hebrew term *domen*, pronounced "doh-men."

5. Some helpful websites, programs, and links: Conquer Series, https://conquerseries.com/; CovenantEyes, http://www.covenanteyes.com/fight-porn-in-your-church/; Pure Life Ministries, https://www.purelifeministries.org/; Paul Maxwell, "Seven Things to Do After You Look at Pornography," Desiring God, March 9, 2016, https://www.desiringgod.org/articles/seven-things-to-do-after-you-look-at-pornography; David Murray, "Top 10 Books on Fighting Porn," HeadHeartHand, May 1, 2014, http://headheart hand.org/blog/2014/05/01/top-10-books-on-fighting-porn/; David Murray, "Top 60 Online Resources for Battling Porn," HeadHeart Hand, May 6, 2013, http://headhearthand.org/blog/2013/05/06/top-60-online-resources-for-battling-porn/. Some helpful books: David Kyle Foster, *Sexual Healing: Reference Edition* (n.p.: Laurus Books, 2018); Steve Gallagher, *At the Altar of Sexual Idolatry* (Dry Ridge, KY: Pure Life Ministries, 2007).

6.   For a classic exposition see D. Martyn Lloyd-Jones, *The Christian Soldier: An Exposition of Ephesians 6:10–20* (Grand Rapids, MI: Baker Books, 1998). For an older, Puritan classic see William Gurnall, *The Christian in Complete Armour* (Peabody, MA: Hendrickson, 2010). For a popular book on breaking strongholds see Neil T. Anderson, *The Bondage Breaker* (Eugene, OR: Harvest House, 2006).

7.   See also Isaiah 11:5, with reference to the Messiah; and Wisdom 5:18 (NRSV), with reference to God.

8.   Peter T. O'Brien, *The Letter to the Ephesians* (Grand Rapids, MI: Wm. B. Eerdmans, 1999), 474, https://www.amazon.com/Letter-Ephesians-Pillar-Testament-Commentary/dp/0802837360.

9.   O'Brien, *The Letter to the Ephesians*, 481.

CHAPTER 12: HOW TO DEFEAT JEZEBEL ON A NATIONAL LEVEL

1.   Cited in David McIntyre, *The Hidden Life of Prayer* (Ross-shire, UK: Christian Focus, 2010), 94.

2.   See 1 Kings 18:1–14.

3.   Charles G. Finney, "The Decay of Conscience," *The Independent of New York*, December 4, 1873, available at The Gospel Truth, http://www.gospeltruth.net/1868_75Independent/731204_conscience.htm.

4.   Tom Gilson, "Church, Wake Up! An Urgent Call to Action," The Stream, December 19, 2018, https://stream.org/church-wake-up-call-to-action/.

5.   Gilson, "Church, Wake Up!"

6.   "AskDrBrown Digital Library," AskDrBrown, accessed April 9, 2019, https://askdrbrown.org/library/.

7.   "Consider This," AskDrBrown, accessed April 9, 2019, https://askdrbrown.org/considerthis/.

8.   You can also get lots of helpful information on a wide range of issues at PragerU, https://www.prageru.com/. For a targeted, thirty-day short-video series hitting on key social issues from an evangelical perspective, go to "Bullseye Challenge," Here's

the Deal Media, accessed April 9, 2019, https://www.heresthedeal
media.com/bullseye-challenge/introduction/.

9. Wang Yi, "Waiting Together for the Day of Redemption"
(sermon, Early Rain Covenant Church, Chengdu, China, September
9, 2018), viewed at Pray for Early Rain Covenant Church, "If Xi Jinping does not repent he will perish!," Facebook, December 29, 2018,
12:54 p.m., https://www.facebook.com/prayforearlyrain/videos
/527784534298136/.

10. Wang, "Waiting Together for the Day of Redemption." See
also Will Maule, "Persecuted Chinese Pastor Calls President Xi Jinping to Repent of His Sins," Faithwire, December 31, 2018, https://
www.faithwire.com/2018/12/31/persecuted-chinese-pastor-calls
-president-xi-jinping-to-repent-of-his-sins/.

11. Lisa Cumming, "Are Jordan Peterson's Claims About Bill
C-16 Correct?," Torontoist, December 19, 2016, https://torontoist
.com/2016/12/are-jordan-petersons-claims-about-bill-c-16-correct/.

12. RobinHoodUKIP, "Jordan Peterson Calmly Dismantles
Feminism Infront of Two Feminists," YouTube, 11:25, May 17, 2018,
https://www.youtube.com/watch?v=Ddzf9Mm4hdY.

13. Izzy Kalman, "The Meteoric Rise of Professor Jordan
Peterson," *Psychology Today*, February 4, 2018, https://www
.psychologytoday.com/us/blog/resilience-bullying/201802/the
-meteoric-rise-professor-jordan-peterson.

14. Amanda Prestigiacomo, "11-Year-Old Boy Dressed in Drag
Dances at Gay Bar, Gets Dollar Bills Thrown at Him," The Daily
Wire, December 17, 2018, https://www.dailywire.com/news
/39409/11-year-old-boy-dressed-drag-dances-gay-men-bar
-amanda-prestigiacomo.

15. "Drag Queen Storytime," Monroe County Public Library,
July 21, 2017, https://mcpl.evanced.info/signup/EventDetails?EventI
d=57096&et=3&backTo=Calendar&startDate=2017/07/01.

16. Todd Starnes, "Gyrating Drag Queen's Erotic Performance
Shocks Audience at Grade School Talent Show," FOX News, June 2,
2017, https://www.foxnews.com/opinion/gyrating-drag-queens
-erotic-performance-shocks-audience-at-grade-school-talent
-show. See also Michael L. Brown, "Here Come the Drag Queens,"
AskDrBrown, June 4, 2017, https://askdrbrown.org/library

/here-come-drag-queens. For a relevant video see Michael L. Brown, "Should Drag Queens Be Reading to Your Toddlers in Libraries?," AskDrBrown, June 3, 2017, https://askdrbrown.org/library/should-drag-queens-be-reading-your-toddlers-libraries. As of this writing, a YouTube video of an eight-year-old drag queen has over 9.6 million views.

17. Starnes, "Gyrating Drag Queen's Erotic Performance Shocks Audience at Grade School Talent Show."

18. Starnes, "Gyrating Drag Queen's Erotic Performance Shocks Audience at Grade School Talent Show."

19. Kate Shellnutt, "Christian Baker Wins Supreme Court's Masterpiece Cakeshop Case," *Christianity Today*, June 4, 2018, https://www.christianitytoday.com/news/2018/june/jack-phillips-masterpiece-cakeshop-wins-supreme-court-free-.html.

20. "About Us," MassResistance, accessed April 9, 2019, https://www.massresistance.org/AboutUs.html.

21. "MassResistance Fight Against 'Drag Queen Story Hour' Targeting Children Goes National," MassResistance, December 12, 2018, https://www.massresistance.org/docs/gen3/18d/Fighting-DQSH-in-NY-AK-MI/index.html.

22. "MassResistance Fight Against 'Drag Queen Story Hour' Targeting Children Goes National," MassResistance. They have a helpful PowerPoint linked in the article as well.

23. Michael L. Brown, "Professor Jordan Peterson Has a Warning From Canada," AskDrBrown, November 9, 2016, https://askdrbrown.org/library/professor-jordan-peterson-has-warning-canada.

24. Brown, "Professor Jordan Peterson Has a Warning /from Canada." See also Jordan B Peterson, "2016/11/16: An update," YouTube, November 5, 2016, https://www.youtube.com/watch?v=BR8tVB7sNxc. Professor Peterson was not dismissed from the University of Toronto as he thought he might be at the time of our interview in 2016.

25. Jordan B Peterson, "Dr. Jordan B Peterson on Femsplainers," YouTube, December 21, 2018, https://www.youtube.com/watch?v=hKUffHXOb8U.

26.   Martin Luther King Jr, *Strength to Love* (Minneapolis: Fortress Press, 2010), 26, https://www.amazon.com/Strength-Love-Martin-Luther-King/dp/0800697405.

27.   See further Michael L. Brown, "What Christian Leaders Can Learn From Donald Trump," AskDrBrown, July 13, 2018, https://askdrbrown.org/library/what-christian-leaders-can-learn-donald-trump.

28.   Mike Hayes, *Renewal: 4 Ways to Change Your Life—and Our Nation* (n.p.: Mike Hayes Ministries, 2018), 126.

29.   Evan Sayet, "He Fights," Townhall, July 13, 2017, https://townhall.com/columnists/evansayet/2017/07/13/he-fights-n2354580.

30.   This was Paul's personal pattern: "Being reviled, we bless. Being persecuted, we endure. Being slandered, we encourage" (1 Cor. 4:12–13). His counsel: "Beloved, do not avenge yourselves, but rather give place to God's wrath, for it is written: 'Vengeance is Mine. I will repay,' says the Lord. Therefore 'If your enemy is hungry, feed him; if he is thirsty, give him a drink; for in doing so you will heap coals of fire on his head.' Do not be overcome by evil, but overcome evil with good" (Rom. 12:19–21, quoting from Deut. 32:35 and Prov. 25:21–22).

31.   Emily Shugerman, "These College Guys Are Trying to Ban Porn on Campus," Daily Beast, December 6, 2018, https://www.thedailybeast.com/these-college-guys-are-trying-to-ban-porn-on-campus.

32.   Shugerman, "These College Guys Are Trying to Ban Porn on Campus."

33.   A. W. Tozer, *Of God and Men* (Chicago: Moody Publishers, 2015), 19.